This copy is for

Sandra McKnight

with my appreciation

and all good wishes —

Victor di Suvero

Santa Fe 2001

HARVEST TIME
SELECTED POEMS 1988 – 2000

Typesetting: Katherine Forrest
Cover Art: Photograph by Victor di Suvero
Typeface: Caslon & Perseus
Method: Direct Disc to Book utilizing Quark program

Library of Congress Card Catalog Number: 00-92752
ISBN: 0-938631-36-5 paper

Thanks to:
Charles Bell, Jack Foley, Thomas Fitzsimmons, Mike Sutin, Barbara Windom,
Jana Edmondson, Ed Santa Ana, Francis Huxley, Henrietta di Suvero,
Herman Berlandt, Charles and Karen Gallenkamp and Lisl and Landt Dennis.

Published by
PENNYWHISTLE PRESS, INC.
P.O. Box 734 Tesuque, NM 87574 USA
email: PennywhistleBook@aol.com

HARVEST TIME
SELECTED POEMS 1988 – 2000
VICTOR DI SUVERO

for Barbara

Table of Contents

Table of Contents

Table of Contents

Note: 🍇 this mark indicates that the poem continues onto the following page.

Here's a gathering, a dozen years of writing around and about the moving to a new world for me, the high desert of the Southwest, a place full of the crowded histories of Indian, Hispanic and Anglo settlers all of whom have called the same stretches of eroded sandstone, harshly cut arroyos and fertile fields and orchards their home.

Pieces of my earlier life, of sea shores and storms and wars and loves lost and found and hopes and dreams are all here along with moments of familial music and of magic found and understandings treasured. These are all here for you, whoever you may be, trusting that a a portion of what I have felt and thought may be shared with you in a manner that will serve you in your passage along the way.

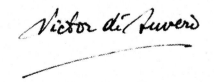

1. LAND & PLACE

For All Of Us

This was the sea once and I walk across the hills,
Down to the arroyo and up again with my eyes
Swimming across the face of a blind escarpment,
Seeing red and ochre bluffs as some strange
Finned creature must have eyed them
When all was water here instead of air and
Another way of being was the way.

I think of that reptilian ancestor whose appetite
For light drove him and his kind to breathe air,
Instead of water. They took possession of the
Land wondering if there was another way to be.

I know that when my children first saw the light
They came out of that same sea and their children
Too, in turn, will rise from there into the air
With perhaps a better chance of finding still
Another way.

This was the sea once and the sun rests on solstice
Night while the midsummer dark is forked
By lightning that charges down the draw,
Driving the huge and crackling thunder into the
Ground reminding us once more that all things
Change, some slowly, and others in a flash.
Always another way to be.

The Land

Whatever is said it was the land that was here first
The crust above the still molten core was and is here;
And whether by virtue of spores carried on the solar wind
Or by the slow progress from single cell to genomes of today
Or by Fiat of Lord Zeus, or Jupiter or JHVH Himself,
Or the Great Mother, we are here now,
Thanks to the shedding of blood.

No child ever born was born
Without blood shed and we continue.

For every field, for every meadow in the world blood has been shed.
In the Old World before Alexander, before Caesar, before Hitler
The blood ran red in the carving of the land, the taking of it.
Here in the Americas before Atahualpa and Cortes, before Oñate
And since then, continuously, the claims of this group or nation
Become boundaries, frontiers, razor wire, walls and fences.

We come and go, flying over Oceans into dreams of Daedalus
Still believing we can carve it up, deed a piece of it to children,
Forgetting that it was always here and will be still
When we are all gone, gone away into the stars while
This planet continues to turn its dawns into nights and not
Remember who we were and what was done here on the land.

Perhaps only the memory of blood
Is all that will remain.

How Did We Come Here?

What was it that drew us here?
Was it the land calling, the piñon?
The great shaped clouds blessing the
Blue of the sky? Was it the dawn's quiet or the
Other one, the one that comes after the day of
Work, at dusk in summer, promising rest and
Respite and all the other good things we dream of
When we let ourselves do so?

How did we come here? Was it the wind? Or was
It the star that moved us, all of us?

Tell me about the Anasazi, how they came here,
Out of the Earth's navel, the Sipapu, the hole in
The ground made by Coyote when Lightning came
After him— tell me about the old ones, the ones
Who came from over the edge by starlight, riding
The wind, driven by hope as well as by terror—
Tell me!

How is it that we came here, to cottonwoods?
We brought our cooking pots
And histories and prayers, we brought our
Hopes to make a place where the children's
Children not yet born may come to tell each other
Stories of how it is that we came here and why—
And they may end up knowing more about it than
We do now.

I have come to give thanks to wind
And star and call of land,
All those that served to bring us here.

Changing The World

"To cut these trees down is to change the world" the old
Man said. *"To cut these trees down means the end—*
"The broken end of three hundred years of growing
"Slowly—summer spurt and autumn holding, winter
"Dreaming and burgeoning of spring—so slow the
"Growth the naked eye will not distinguish rings
"When looking at the cut."

                  The quarter acre being
Cleared counted eighteen piñon among the juniper.
Of these, ten were older than the nation's
History, three had seen the light before the
Pueblos threw the Spaniards back south and out of
Here. In a summer's day on the quarter acre
Reaching up towards the sky, dancing with the
Wind nodding yes and no and touching tenderly
The piñon rustled their farewells.

And now the trees are three cords of wood down
On the ground, stacked four feet tall. No longer
Haven of the raven or the magpie or the finch but
Promise of warmth in winter with the land cleared
And graded for the building yet to come.
"Yes—the world is changed" the old man said—

"The ghosts of those piñon will always be with us,"
He said, waving his arms slowly turning in the
Small afternoon breeze.

Field Stuff

You reap what you sow all right but the other
Elements of the equation must be there
Too.
             The land has to be
Tilled, prepared and made ready for the
Seed—which, once sown, has to be nurtured,
Watered, kept free of pests and permitted to
Sprout into the light. Then cared for until its
Fullness becomes an eagerness to be shared—

Yes, then you know the harvest, not before.
The images you see on pages of the catalogs
Identify the crops others have raised.
Your crop is witness to what you have done
With that which has been given you.

Talent, clarity, strength and persistence, a
Sense of humour to save you when required,
Willingness to share and a recognition of the
Light are for us as sun and water are to
The grain and corn and vegetables we grow.

To Be Here

When the sun reaches its stopping place having
Gone as far North as it ever does, we all breathe
That sigh that says *"It will come back down again!*
"It will!"

And then miracles begin to happen, berries turn,
The winter's rabbits move more quickly, the light
Begins to change even though we know we will
Have still more ice and snow to face.

The year's wheel begins to turn forward again and
Each one of us finds ways to manage and to move
Again toward Spring and its miracles even as we
Turn to deal with the biting cold.

Smoke rises in the slow dark evening air. the deer
Tracks and the coyote's are both elegant in white.
Reasons for loving come again and gentleness
Touches the light of stars.

Hope is born in a manger and oil lamps burn
Beyond their time. The piñon and cedar steady
Their places on the mountain's side and life looks
As if it will come shining again.

I have spent all my life learning to be here this night,
This moment, by this fire, waiting for the future
To come, to bring us all to ourselves first
Then to each other and then to song.

In The Early Spring

Imagine the work the roots do when the
Ground thaws and the radicle begins to
Swell and the rootlets go out first as hair
Thin explorations, then filling out while in
The dark, growing with no air but purpose,
With no light but the need to feed the plant
Above that will flower in the sun in time.

The work the roots do is silent— it
Generates no appreciation or applause. The
Roots serve and feed the plant they are a
Part of—and the flowering becomes seed,
Which falls into the ground to round the
Cycle once again with light into another
Time, another growing, serving the entirety,
Silent as the stretch of time.

I see my children going out into the world
Raising their wings into the air as I pray the
Wind to ease their landings here on an earth
Carpeted with grass and flowers all of which
Would not be there without the work that
Roots have done.

II. TIME & LIGHT

What Is Your Name?

Who are you,
Saint of the near miss, the close call?
Turning the car's wheel,
Deflecting the knife's point
So that we walk out of the hospital
The next day greeting the sun
Gratefully?

What are you, guardian angel,
Kachina, invisible spirit and friend,
You—the one who makes the judge
Hear our side of the case, who
Drops the name from the list,
Wakes the lookout on time
And makes one miss the train
That connected with the plane that goes down?

I build you this poem at dawn
Gratefully listening to the squawking of jays,
To the sound of water falling
And to the intermittent silence
Wondering how it is that so few
Know you, acknowledge you, praise you,
Saint of the near miss, the close call.

Time Is All We Have

It is really all we have, to give, to use, to
Share with the beloved. Time is all we have
Given to us as long as body's strength
Permits us life—all else does not belong
To us—stewards of one kind or another,
Caretakers or wastrels, good ones,
Bad ones and some in between, solitary,
Gregarious, committed to a cause or to
Acquisitions, we share this passage we call time
While doing all the other things we do.

We sleep, sing, dance and work, bring
Children into the world while undoing
Enemies as well as animals and birds.
With each and every act of ours we use
Pieces of our capital without remorse.
Every single thing takes time—sleep
Takes time, stupidity as well—the one
Argument for the good life is economy
Achieved by not wasting time on guilt,
Regrets or even penances.

                Time's faces, the dark
One and the light, are the faces of our
Lives—sad and somber, serious and
Wondrous, bright and full of laughter,
From one moment to another when we
Notice their reflections
In our lives.

Timing

"It's not time, yet." She said, indicating that a
Certain time would come when every single thing
Would be perfect and appropriate and birds
Wearing their best plumage would break into
Song and all the fruit trees in the garden
Would send perfumes and promises of sweetness
Into the air.

       "It's not time, yet!" She said again as
Eve must have said before the apple ripened, as Peter
Must have thought before the cock crowed thrice, as even
Cleopatra is said to have said to her handmaiden when
She brought the basket with the asp inside.

             It is the
Balancing of time that is the greatest art. The fencer
Has to know the exact instant when the avenue
To his opponent's heart is open so as to be able to thrust
And win. The singer has to learn to hold that one
Note for ever and learn not to let it go before its time
To make it right. Even the bartender about to shut
His shop, no matter how anxious he might be to be
On his way home, when asked, if it's not right, will say
"No, it's not time, yet, but it will be soon," and on that
Perception we all rely having learned that timing is
As important as time itself and more than any other
Single thing for when its wrong cars collide, hearts
Break, futures are lost, children die and worlds
Fall in upon themselves.

This Time

This time is different always from that time.
Chronometer, Greenwich Mean Time,
Sidereal Time, Once upon a Time and Time
To Think are all different from That Time.

Every Day Time, Time Clock Time, Time To
Check In Time and One More Time are
Other kinds yet again and not That Time,
Because That Time is the one of the beloved.

The one that takes us out of time,
Into eternity in which there is no
Before or after where one can look
And see that what was, is and will be;

And that all of it was, is and will be
Now and that the entire manufactory
Of the past worked industriously to
Make it possible for us to be here now
Completely drenched by the persistence
Of the Moment which only comes to life
When I touch your hand in this way
Differently than I ever have before
Making me, finally, able to change time.

Winter Solstice

This is when the great wheel of the year
Dips down. When the sun shines the trees in the
North at noon when the deer's breath and the
Hare's breath and the dog's breath cloud the cold
With their small handfuls of steam. This is the time
When the cross exists only in the outstretched
Arms of the winter's tree
And the child in each of us is born once more.

This is when the great wheel in the sky
Dips down to fill its iron clawed bucket with
Bundles of hope for the year and the dreams nestle
Down and the night is at bay and the touch of a
Hand becomes a smile. This is the time when the
Pain of the world is held for a moment only in the
Arms of those who care
And the child in each of us is born once more.

This is when the great wheel of the world
Dips down. When the wave spume becomes ice as
The wind takes the salt drops to give them shape
For a moment before dropping them once again
Into hard driving sea to melt. This is the time
When so many of those ready to die choose to go into
The space between the stars
And the child in each of us is born once more.

This is when the great wheel of the stars
Dips down. When the Pleiades come close and the
Great Bear shines when the summer's fruit and
The winter's grain join in the faith that Spring will
Come and be light again. This is the time that
Forgives the hurt, that sings and praises
And the child in each of us is born once more.

Sounds That Made Us Well Before

Even grown men with all their faculties in full fettle need
To hear from time to time what they heard as children
When they were growing up from their mothers, sisters,
Aunts, nurses or other caregivers that it was all right or
That it would be and not to worry before one went to
Sleep and even when the words themselves are not heard
But their echo is evoked so that they imagine they can
Hear those words once again, the ones they heard an
Eternity ago. They come back like the brushing of the
Wings of the cherubim that used to come into their
Nights instead of the piercing of airport noises and
Highway lights.

Going to sleep alone is a lot like dying must be, the
Letting go, even with the family around the bed or the
Swirl of voices and of disconnected colors in the
Emergency room or even in the car's crash or the bullet's
Thud which is why I suppose some of us will do just
About anything to avoid that going to sleep by one's own
Self, even putting up with a bad marriage, a worse
Relationship or even being part of a ship's crew or
Finding a homeless shelter or even jail where other
Bodies with a sense of life can be sensed to breathe and
Murmur and toss and turn together in company as in the
Old days when life was truly communal, when we were
Like cubs in a litter or part of the young in a tribe, all
Together in a tent or cave or shelter, even under the
Open sky—a reason for sleepovers and camping
These days.

We go to sleep alone each night, even with someone next
To our tired selves practicing for the long one, the one
From which none of us will wake, listening for those
Sounds, those words that made us well before.

Time Teaches

Time teaches us to serve the arts
As acolytes are trained. Some of us
Simply remain there, in training,
Raising money, sending newsletters out
Into the world, forgetting to graduate,
Forgetting the one point of it,
The joy of being and of this
World we can enjoy with smiles.

It's all here in this high desert:
A daughter's wedding coming in the Fall,
The sound of hooves drumming on the wind,
The wry smile of a friend dead too soon of AIDS,
The working dreams of a new house
While politicians play their shabby games.
The winds of friendship are serene and good and
Even Othello Simpson's looming presence on CNN
Does not undo our sense of right
As the Spring's first crocus springs
Into the hands of lovers
And children run to play—
                              Learning
A piece of music can teach us how to hear
The cantata of the streets, the odes of clouds
And the songs immanent in the voice
Of the beloved.
                    In a film, "The Madness
"Of King George," it is Cordelia's speech
To her Dad, sweet, impossible and mad
Old Lear; and then her kiss upon his cheek
That heals the King.
                              Poetry does serve all
Of us—even as the seasons and the horses do—
As lovers serve each other in the night of days
And in the day of nights while time
Teaches us to serve as we go along our ways.

Now and Today

It's been fifty years since V-J day came down.
It's a lifetime that's gone by—and we're still here
To talk about the random acts and flukes that
Made the difference for each one of us.

Now it's not easy to call up the fear that
Caught us in the gut when the General
Alarm rang out—not easy to remember
The pungent smell the fifty millimeter shells
Made in the gun tub aft as they came pouring
Out of the machine—not easy to stand lookout
Once again boring holes in the solid darkness of
The night to see the possibility of death each
Watch we stood in convoy or alone.

                            Today I found the
Bundled letters I had written home when I was
Out there in the Pacific. *"I hope and trust you're*
"All well and we're fine out here" was the way the
First letter closed—how fine was fine and what
Is it that we knew then and not now?

It's a lifetime that's gone by and teachers I have
Had have taught me that the *"Now"* is the only
Point in time we can be certain of, and I have
Not learned that lesson very well because the
Past crowds in and the future's down there
Knocking at the gate and it all runs by as
Quickly as a meteor does when it comes into
Our atmosphere.

                          Now I only know I sit
Here remembering and wondering who that
Person was who wrote those letters and signed
My name.

And I Could Have Been One Of Them

The snow fell all night last night. This
Morning, walking through it, the half mile
Down the hill to get the Sunday paper and
Back up as the cold mist turned the world
Into black and white like those old photos
Of the war in Russia, I understood in a new way
How it must have been for the boys in that
Division of the Italian Army green at
16 and 17, sent up to the Russian Front
By Mussolini, at Hitler's demand.
Stalingrad.

Out of the sunbaked hill towns, the groves
Where lemons, oranges and olives came from,
The untrained fodder for the Russian guns
Went, ill-clothed, with gloves so thin
The fingers froze. The sixty thousand men
And officers of the Blue Division turned blue
And died—all but eleven hundred and sixty-two,
Who somehow managed to make it through
And get back to Italy.

Fifty-four years have gone by and it's all
One now, even the memory. Fifty-eight
Thousand and some may not be so many, but
The stupidity of even one event like that in
The light of the millions dead freezes the heart.

How will I be able to tell my children how stupid
This generation of ours has been and how
Stupidly this waste keeps on wasting us all away,
In Afghanistan, in Israel, in Florida and in the town
Next door as it did in 'Nam and now Rwanda,
Sierra Leone, Timor and the high desert
Where we now live.

Light

In every dream of Heaven
There is always that brilliance
And that wanting to go there—
Always toward the light—
Even the seed in the dirt pushes
Up into the light and air—

Coyote's pups crawl out of
Their burrow, out into the world
To move into their light and
Ours where we can be at one
With the sun and where
At night the stars come out
For all to see and to be with.

From Ahknaton on
The Light and
The Idea of God
Have been one.

Dante's vision and the stars
Still blaze here tonight while
I fumble, looking for a match.

A Canticle For Today

Trip, travel, voyage, expedition to the
Antipodes with or without provisions,
Clothed always with surprise, we all appear
To move into discovery, dance with delight
And wonder, crowding experience as we go.

No one had told you that parakeets would fly
Yellow into blue green jungles to lead you
Into difficult tangles of lianas and
Relationships. No one had taught you to
Keep your head and your silver sense of
Balance while threading your way over future
Cataracts and chasms.

No one had told you lions were there ready
To eat you if you stumbled, and that in the
Hot sands of anger all things put on realities
That do not belong to them.

Changing truths move as the rays of light
Reflected from the mirrored dance hall ball
Above the couples moving in and out on the
Slippery floor. These rays shine for a
Fractioned instant only
Throwing light into the air.

And you learn, you learn each day,
To take one step at a time,
To hope, to pray, to breathe,
To find your way out of the labyrinth.

Grain By Grain

Looking hard into that instrument by which some of us
Measure time, I fix upon that space through which the
Grains of sand drop from the goblet shape into its other
Self below. It has no name at all. The centuries
That dropped through that nameless place
Could have become Gobi, Sahara or
That forlorn and magical stretch of
Those Peruvian coastal dunes
I know. All those uncounted
Grains falling through that
Aperture that divides the
Future from the Past!
"hole" or even
"drop,"
Still
The job of
Naming it will
Change it not at all,
Each grain of sand will
Find its way into and through
This space. Its disengagement from
The mass above becomes engagement
In bulking up of that growing mountain
Down below. It gives itself permission to enter
And go through that nameless space, and, while
Falling, it turns into a love, a life, a child—each
Grain no more than this one moment, this piece of paper,
This pen with which I write, this day with all its complications,
This network of muscle, nerves, and blood, which makes me up
This life of mine, grain by grain, through the nameless place of now.

The Two Cousins

Time and love are kin. Both are intangible
And yet touch and shape each and every thing
We do. Each stretches out to distances unseeable
While holding within themselves the power to bunch up,
Creating chaos in their folds as in this piece of
Crumpled paper. Yes, each one lives in all we do
And becomes even more noticeable when either leaves
Our lives and disappears.
                      When time stops for us, we die.
When love stops we may not die immediately, but often
Wish we had.
              However, when time sings for us and all
Its moves are somersaults of bright delight, it's really quite
The same as when we fall in love, head over heels in love,
Heeding the gentle push that nature gives us when we see
A candidate, a likely mate with whom we'd make
A perfect child—and odd how we think it's our free
Will at work when it's only the old wise Mother
Saying, *"Yes, that one would do for you"*—and then,
There is the time for it, the time that makes it happen

Dance, sing, and play while one loses all sense of time,
Discovering the pleasures of forevers.

They are indeed kin to each other, these two. They
Frame the world in which you and I can be together;
Lose one, and you've lost the other.

Ulysses in Tesuque

On that shore far away
After the ring of blood
Had been filled and after
The other shades had come and gone
It was Tiresias
Who told me I would find
Peace and rest in the mountains —
If I were to go inland so far, he said,
That a wayfarer I would meet
Would ask the use of the oar
I would be carrying on my shoulder.
"Would that be a winnowing flail?"
He'd ask, and then I'd set it down,
Make my sacrifice to Poseidon,
And find my peace at last —

And I did that — and I did plant
My oar here and built a house —
But the grapes of my desire
Were not made into wine
And the roses in the garden
Are beaten down by summer hail
While dreams of soft sand,
Salt spume and sea shells merge
With the talk of old compañeros
Remembering all the voyages
And the long way home.

All those things consume my nights
And eat the marrow of the years
I've left to breathe — not knowing
If the thunder roars to send me on,
Back to the sea or to keep me here
Until that night that has no dawn
Comes with its mirror to find me out.

After Rilke

Be ahead of all leave takings
As though they were all behind you
Just as the summer that is no more
Is behind you with all its fruit and flowering.

Be ready each day with farewell so that
You may always arise with surprise
Into that seamless song soaring far
Beyond the heavens and into the stars.

Be,

Knowing the great void where all things begin,
The infinite source of all that moves,
So that you may be at one with Light.

For all that which is used up,
Done in, turned out, give thanks;
It all served to bring you here.

III. HEART TALK

Question

What makes us willing?
What is the will—the one that makes us
Fall in love?
Fall out of bed?
Fall down?
Fall?
Did it all begin with that?
The Fall—Garden of Eden?
That autumn when the apple
First ripened on the tree
Is it that which gets us every time?

When she wills—is willing—
And we fall
In love, in and out of bed.
Down—fall?
Is it that
Always as a matter of will?
When she wills
Then we males
Serve that force
Thinking it is
Our will.

Stuff Of Life

The making of love, not to be confused with
The satisfaction of an appetite or the
Conscious begetting of a child, even though
All three modes may co-exist, requires at least
As much care as the making of a loaf of bread
Whose ingredients have been gathered and
Kneaded together in appropriate order, set to
Rise and then baked to send rich aromas into
Air, so that when done, it can be shared and
Enjoyed while earning its proper name and
Turning us into its acolytes and celebrants!

                           But wait!

What is it then that drives us to kill others of
Our kind because of differences we may have
About our Heavens and what we have to do
To get there? What is it that puts peace and
Happiness at risk at every turn?

                      Is it not always a lack of
Love or lack of bread, or even a lack of both
Together? In spite of all, my trust lives in the
Baking of the bread and the baring of
The heart.

That Which Is Reasoned

That which is reasoned belongs, justly, to the rational;
To philosophers, to teachers, and to lawyers.

That which is poetry transcends the atomic table,
Fibonacci's curve and the steps that
Lead us from here to there.

        It is not Reason
That sings in the songs of ecstasy.

It is not Reason that moves the heart and takes
Spirit and the skylarks dancing.

Reason and its orders make up the essence of
The car you drive, the phone you ring to
Be with the beloved, where you arrived
Yesterday with an armful of daffodils,
Fresh baked loaves of crusty bread and
Wine and laughter with no reason at all
Except the underlying one of life itself, its
Its appetites, its laughter and its joy
Of being there.

From The Barbara Poems

Sleeping spoonlike
Even the spirit
Rests before
Stirring dawn
Into a froth
Of pale light

    The beach sings
    At low tide
    Not even
    The strident gulls
    Disturb
    Its melody

Pelicans perforate
The evening sky
As if to permit us
To tear a roseate
Piece to keep
At home like this

    The brave part
    Reaches out
    To help
    The wise part
    Protects
    And prays

There are days
Divided
By a river
Of distances
When I need her
She calls

I dredge up
Left over gems
To find one
Worthy of her
All I find
Is my heart

    I am more
    Sure than ever
    And more
    Unsure
    At the same time—
    Learning to pray

No compromise
Is permitted
In her house
The false note
Is barred and
Bad lamps exiled

    Her memories
    Make her wince
    When we talk—
    My past also
    Sometimes when
    We are silent

Under the tent
Inside
With no secrets
Connected again
We hold each other
And are well

The water
The pool holds
Her tenderly
While I envy
Its ability
To caress her

    The idea
    Of other bodies
    Still surfaces
    I am so
    Glad after
    To find hers

She dreams
The best for me
I dream
Everything for her
After which
Reality stings

    Everything I have
    I brought to her—
    There was a lot
    I would rather
    Have left behind
    But could not

All the things
Not done chatter
Like the birds
Playing brickball
In the roof gravel
At dawn

    The children came
    To visit us
    Surprised we
    Had found
    New ways
    And smiled

She could not
Bear to hear
Old stories
Of unfinished pain
And yet she
Suffered them quietly

    We turned away
    Inland to build
    A new house
    In high desert
    Remembering incense
    Beginning again

The Same Thing

It is the same thing that drives the stallion
To mount the willing mare standing there
In the meadow winking and waving her tail
As if to say "I'm here for you, big boy."

                                        It is
The same thing that drove Mark Anthony and
Caesar to want the power of Empire so as to have
That which each one wanted—

                              The same thing
That drove Henry the Eighth into those paroxysms
Of lust and fury that divided England from Rome—
Always the same down to our time when
Another King of England threw his Empire to the wind
For the whetting of his appetites—

                         We are an odd lot
Inventing grand towering names for that feeling
That comes over us as it came over King David
When he saw Bathsheba bathing on her roof
That summer's afternoon not so long ago
Causing murder and betrayal in the palace.

It's the same thing that's made women careless
And men foolish since it all began, yes, the same
Thing that moves the finches and the other
Birds to build their nests in Spring—that makes
The white tailed doe stand quivering in Autumn
In the high meadows of this mountain range.
The same thing that fuels all the attention given
To the development of abs and quads in health clubs
Across the country and the marketing of creams,
Of clothes, of perfumes and of dreams so as to enhance
The desirability of each and every one of us.

LOVE, The Word

In Alaska the Inuit have more than
Thirty names they use for snow and
The scientists at Los Alamos use
Even more specific appellations to
Identify the various states of matter
So as to get the correct handle for
Which function of which state they mean;
And money too has been recognized by
A wide variety of names from the shekel
Of the Bible to the Drachma, the Lira,
Franc and Pound and to the Dollar and
The Electronic Money Transfers of today.

Isn't it odd then that we who use this
English tongue have only one word for that
Most variable of feelings—
                              It's that word
LOVE, that's overworked, that means
Too many things, that has to be given
Qualifiers and modifiers and adjectives
And adverbs to mean any single thing
At all—filial and familial, of country
And of God—of food and of the beloved,
Puppy and desperate and eternal and
Of cats and horses and of the universe
All crowding into those four letters
That embrace our relatives, our neighbors,
Manifestations of the Spirit and, of course,
Our individual, singular and lonely selves.

It Is Possible

The rehabilitation of a heart ill used and wasted
Requires willingness and the suspension of disbelief.
The continuing surges of misplaced appetites and
The need for gratification now must be excised,
Old ways put aside and, though quite difficult,
The blackboard has to be cleaned and cleared.

Old ways of pulling away from the world, retreats,
Convents or monasteries, the lonely walk out into
The desert or the desolation of a threadbare room
With a naked bulb for light at night, bathroom
Down the hall at one end, in a downtown hotel, or
Hunkering down beside a small fire in the forest are
All ways of initiating the voyage back to clarity.

It is possible, though difficult to believe, that heart
Will heal. New muscle will grow back; scar tissue
Becomes less fierce with time; though forgiveness,
Particularly of the self, is a required element.

Having done so many things that will not stand
Dawn's light or even become the subject of
A discussion with a trusted friend there is no
Way to go forward without belief. Faith in
The possibility of a good outcome is absolute
As a requirement. Heartsick yearning for
The time when all was well only delays
The process of recovery.
                              Faith is needed to
Dig and turn the earth, making it ready
For the seed to be planted once again,
Trusting that the crop will grow clean this time
And harvest time will come and the hurt
Be remembered only as a place one will not
Need to visit any more.

The Air Touches Her

—*after Patchen*

The air touches her everywhere
And music bathes her while
Her eyes are brushed by brilliant
Coruscations and the colors of the dawn.

Drawn out of her body's secret places
Her spirit sings its possibilities and
Finds answers full of pleasures to
The questions posed by her realities.

She manages to weave both past
And future into the fabric of a cloth
Which we have learned to shape
Into the bright banners of the present.

When she comes home to me after
Having been away, it is Spring again
No matter what the weather
Or the season of the year!

To Be Loving

To be loving is to discover reasons for life.
To be loving is to wake wonders and make
Gentleness descend with the Spring's rain.
To be loving is to forgive the past, embrace
The possible and enhance the colors of dawn.
To be loving is to enclose entire languages
In a gesture and oceans of desire in a look.
To be loving is to discover patience as a way
Of life, not as a game, nor as a trial
To be undergone without anxiety or fear.
To be loving is to recognize that the sole
Of the most beautiful foot is most beautiful
Because it supports beauty with each step
Along every road and remains true and
Constant even when it is tried by walking on fire.

To be loving one must reach into corners
One did not know existed in one's own heart
And choose to make order in the jumble usually
Found there. To be loving one must be as brave
As one can possibly be or else the battle is lost
Before it is joined and satisfaction will flee.
To be loving one must learn to hear, not
Just to listen, to distinguish, not just to see
Or count up the items presented by life.

To be loving one must learn to receive, to
Accept and to understand as well as
To give, to offer, to share and to teach.
To be loving one must come to the moment
Untrammeled by baggage, without fear
Of the consequences, with the sure knowledge
That of all the stars in the heavens
The one lighting this moment is the only
One whose light counts and is impeccable.

Goddess Flesh

Sunset in August, the purple mountains
And the August rain—he turned
Not knowing where he had landed,
Where he was, where he touched or
Whom—had never felt such smooth
Response to fingers tip, not at the
Louvre on Nike's skin, not on early
Peaches in the orchards' trees.
                                     No—he
Had not touched sunlight at dusk
Or translated young apricots at dawn
Before—he had not known the runner's
Plane of muscle at the hip to be
Like that—Yes, his son's quads and
His daughter's gardening arms—
The cherrywood bowl he had shaped
And finished almost a century ago were fine
But not like this understanding
Of the spirit turned into Flesh—
As in the beginning when the Word
Itself was made Flesh—like this.

The body made into the container,
The housing, the manifestation of
The spirit in the August rain and
He took that clarity with him to
Remember always August sunset,
August rain and the spirit's touch.

On Investigation

How does the heart open?

Is it like a book that can be taken down
    from a shelf and opened to a passage
    one has known and loved?

Is it like a rose opening to the sun an
    hour after dawn to celebrate the day
    attracting bees and humming birds to life?

Does the heart open in the same way that
    we open the door to the house we live in
    when we get there after long journeys?

Does the heart know to prepare for the
    opening of itself to wonder and delight?

Does the heart take stock and does it
    make itself ready to open only when the
    time is right and ripe?

Will we ever know how it is that the
    heart does know and always recognizes the
    right time to do its trick and open?

Like now—

The Prize

Those who go looking for it seldom seem to find it.
Those who have their faces and their bodies carved
Into that which they believe will be more attractive
Lose it.

Those who cannot find it in their own hearts
Never seem to find it in the hearts of others.
                                    The wind
Will bring it, sometimes; at other times it's the rain or
An unexpected stranger at the door.
                                    When found
And not recognized it becomes mist and disappears.

Tentative as well as bold, demanding, stubborn as a
Mule can be at times, and also generous and even
Forgiving, it lives through tragedy and loss and
Will be there to hold the hand and caress
The old man's hair and touch the child and make
The house bright and the lark sing.
                                    It will
Even serve to bring time to stop and the future
Into a place where it can be shaped—but try
To force it into any canister or box and it flies
Away never to return.
                                    We all know its habits
And its ways—odd that we rarely seem to know
What to do with it when it decides to come and stay.

To Live With The Beloved

To live with the beloved
One does not rely solely
On mystic connections
The brilliant dance of the flowers
The understandings of never before
The sweat of delight in the bed
Or the stillness of sunset
When the wind has died down
And there is food in the house.

To live with the beloved
One does not leap into
Dangerous waters, quicksand,
Or otherwise risk life and soul
Without concern, play cards
With the devil, give up
Discourse, run with the crowd,
Retire into deserts and solitude
Or bark at the moon dismayingly.

To live with the beloved
One must learn to be up
With the dawn for its blessings
To wash dishes as sacrament
To clean the house in ways
That are luminous, to sing
And fetch and follow through and
Tend to the tangible, maintaining
The body in balance with spirit.

Otherwise the days are numbered, the sand
Is measured out, the fabric tears, expressions
Ring hollow, the bud withers, and one is not
There at all.

Again

Blood stays quiet, does not race ahead
Does not make for roaring in the ear
When there's mending to be done,
When it's cleanup time,
When there's fixing and patching
And putting the storm windows up or down
And writing the duty letters,
And all that tidying up to be done.

No rush when the stuffed routine
Runs from door to store
And then runs out again,
Repetition being the one ingredient
That can always put one to sleep as in
Piece work, factory, sorting, counting,
Counting, folding, counting, boring.

And yet we can not forget
The other side of that "Again,"
The one that happens when the sun shines
When the mountains sing, when birds
Do cartwheels, when roses jump into their blooms
And when the heart goes riding through long
And yellow fields of hope and one turns
To the beloved saying, *"Yes, sweet one,*
"Again, yes, again, again, again!"

Yes

To speak of love is dangerous
Unless praise and the long view
Be also on the tongue —
To speak of love when passion's fire
Heats up the boiler of the blood
Seduces only those who would be seduced
Even without words.

To speak of love is to learn to touch the stars,
Bend all the winds and laze along
The whale's course in the cold streams
That flow down the California coast
To the warm pastures of our salty dreams.

To speak of love is also sweet and foolish,
Something we all do when the sap rises
And then even a young bureaucrat becomes eloquent
Singing of silks and distant saffron dreams
As if love had been invented that day at nine.

But to speak of love with the beloved
In the tent of pleasure with mingled breath,
When time dissolves and words give way to touch
And all the senses merge into discovery and sweat
One only needs that one word "Yes."

"Yes" to the shedding of the sheets of sleep while
Waking once again together with the sun
So that legs and eyes and hair and hands
All weave themselves into a tapestry
That encompasses the world.

That one word "Yes" on fire again,
Yes.

IV. OUR TRADE

Our Work

We deal in surprises. Our magic
Turns words into delights or tears.
We remind, recall and represent.
With us complaints become eloquence
And when anger is vented by us even
Revolutions can be fired up by
What we do.
                Lonely and alone even
While dancing or whipping up a crowd
We give people reasons to fall in love,
To rediscover the universe, and to
Learn about hope in winter—yes, and
To believe even in themselves.

Our own experience becomes a
Mirror for all those who read
And hear our work.
                   Older than
Iron mongers we are those whose
Craft was learned in caves even
Before the great temples were
Raised to honor Ishtar and Isis.

We praise Orion and sing for
The Seven Sisters remembering
To see even when blinded and
To hear even when we are deaf
So as to be voice and vanguard
For all that happens here.

Questions

"Why do you write?" "What made you decide?"
"Why do you persist?" "How did you get started?"
"What drove you to it?" "Does it ever pay?"

The poet is seen as someone strange,
An apparition, of no earthly use,
Someone who hears voices, sees visions,
Feels tremors caused by battles fought
Between armies of the day
And armies of the night.

Perhaps that's why
So many of us decide to hide in academies
Playing the roles of teachers to the young,
Hoping to eat and not be noticed
While doing the work
Necessary as blood,
Indispensable as water.

There are certain kinds of glues that hold broken
Toys together, or bits of a glass bowl, or lives—
Glues that become transparent
When they harden to hold things together.

Perhaps that is all that poetry is—
A way of fixing what breaks,
A way of invisibly mending what's not right,
A way of saying "Yes"
To all questions.

Perhaps also a way of answering each other
In ways that will not wound or kill.

Empty Words

And they say we use empty words
They say *"Your words are empty,*
"They do not hold a thing. It's only
"Living flesh that counts – the unique person
"Standing there in front of you." And yet

All of us are interchangeable.
Queen Isabella's skull and Montezuma's
Look mightily the same today
And all the world's magnificence
Fades into gray as we go on.

It is not bone and muscle that remain,
Not tongue, not brain, but words alone
That sing and come back again with
Tears and joy and pride and tenderness
To shine and shape our days.

We are blessed with voices; let us then
Praise it all, even the pain, the bad choices
And the falling rain; praising fish
And birds and children out at play
Knowing that our empty words are still
The only keepers of our lives.

Our Poems

They converse with the sun,
Take the moon out dancing
And deal with the stars as friends.

Our poems destroy boundaries,
Include even the exclusive
And permit enemies to share
Our aspirations as well as our doubts.

Our poems have holes in their socks
As well as wings at their heels;
They bear discomfort and splendor
And curiosity on their shoulders.

They acknowledge the lineage of Neruda and Whitman
And embrace all others from Adam to Zulu.
Our poems are as concerned about the cry of a child
As they are about the turn of a phrase.

Our poems travel the road of the painful,
Delve into despair, know death and disasters
Without drowning or sinking.
Our poems are survivors, on disks, on paper,
In minds tuned to the future.
Our poems do not diminish.
Our poems honor the fallen, the weak,
The crazies and wanderers,
Those with no home in our houses.

They converse with the sun,
Take the moon out dancing
And establish themselves
With the stars.

On The Path Of Light

—for Rudolfo Anaya

Treading lightly on the path we choose, we
Acknowledge fortune with each step we take.

When we lose our way we drop into the dark.
When we forget ourselves or what
We've learned, we become shadows,
Lacking substance, fragments of that dark.

To have the courage to permit the sun
To bring its clarity into our souls
Is laudable and brilliant. To keep it there
Takes dancing as well as dedication, takes
Laughter as well as that extra distance that
We may have to run along that path.

The dark is necessary, we know, and
There are many that choose that way
Of going, but the trees and rivers,
The stones and mountains, the sky
And clouds are all vibrant in the light.

To be one with the sun
On the side of life
Is not always the easy one.

Letter To Agostinho Neto

I have translated your poems for seven years
Taken your angers and your tears out of one bucket
And put them into another
And they're there, but they don't wash

I have translated your poems for seven years
Gone to bed with your despair in the night's black
And gotten up with your hope at dawn
And they're there, but I can't talk

I have translated your poems for seven years
Before you became President and a beacon
Lighting the way for your people
And for us, but neither quietly nor gently

It is always hard to carry anything heavy
Logs for the railroad
A memory, even a country

Night Questions

Poet—Facing you in the mirror
Poet—Alone with your heart
Poet—Concentrating on the keyboard
Poet—Rhyming while driving
Poet—Who are you but your own self?

On this hand only the latest practitioners
Discovering new ways to say the old things,
Eagerly dressing up in new clothes, new hats,
While on the other hand, the old ways
Of reaching into the mind to move tears
Into eye, and to move blood into the throat.

Lighthouse keeper, tailor, pilot, programmer,
Hunter, hermit, painter, fencer, dancer,
You who do it alone, by your lone selves,
Walking the cold paths at the top of the world
Are all kin to eagle, to hawk and to falcon
And also kin to asp and to serpent rattler.

Voice of the vision, bringer of promise
Guide for tomorrow, lover of mornings
Window of pleasure, measure of salt,
Histories' carrier, memory's pawn,
Who are you but your own self!

Yes, go look in the mirror
Again.

The Fortunate Ones

In many ways they are fortunate—those who do
Not dream of defying death by virtue of some
Notable adventure, circumnavigating the globe,
Flying to the Moon or to Mars or other stars for
The first time, building great edifices to honor gods
Or even sculptures that stand to teach and please
The populace or conquer nations, sicknesses or
Hunger—those whose vision is
Circumscribed by the boundaries of their
Circumstance, the frontiers of their village, the
Work they have been taught to do and like; who
Are satisfied and pleased by the consistent texture,
And the appearance of the bread they bake, the
Carpets they weave, the embroideries they stitch
And the glass they blow.

Then there are others who try to embrace
A life that is sensible, at least in appearance, who
Also try to defy death by writing—by writing
Poems, songs, novels and histories by which they
Hope and trust to be remembered by others,
Unknown and yet to be born, as having lived to be
The author of this text or that one, and that by
Doing so, have enlarged the world for others, all
The others, who one day will come and say "Oh,
"Yes, him," or perhaps, "her I remember," and in that
Way overcome mortality leaving a bit more than a
Tombstone to mark their passing along this road.

                    I have not yet discovered
Whether the choice of one way or the other is
Conscious and wonder if we are driven to the path
We take or are dropped randomly by the Fates into
One can or another by Chance herself.

Poets At Lunch

—for Thomas Fitzsimmons and Ron Chalmers

Three white crows tell each other stories.
Their own and those of others—stories of when
Their feathers were black and shining as their
Beaks were sharp around their appetites.
Sibilant seniors now, these poets who had
Been around the world and town and
Had not yet been ground down like so
Many of their kind had been. Three
Old young men shaping their memories,
Echoing music and smiles and laughs
For each other, daring even to remember
Things not said to anyone else across
The years, the table or even the bed, touching
The cold of ocean and the sweat and stink
And sting of jungle and of that rot that
Eats feet and groin and open wounds as
Easily as it eats time, machinery and life.

Three of us talking about how we had learned
We had to work together to shape a day or
Even an hour at a time and how we,
Coming from such different places, had
Come to learn there was only one place
Called Quiet that had no attendant
Consciousness at all from which we came.

Each one of the three of us still so full of plans
Of dreams and wantings that underneath
The white of the long wing feathers the black
Showed to be still there to push us along.
Having learned to be silent as well as how
To sing, having learned to catch an updraft
As well as how to beat our now white wings
And also having learned that all the stories
Are still the same as they were then, we
Now know that we can still stride out
Into the sun of this winter afternoon
To live the rest what is left to us to live
As if it were springtime and the dawn.

Discoveries

—for Chungliang Al Huang

My Chinese brother arrives with his retinue.

A prince of the kingdom of movement, with his students,
His musicians, his admirers his acrobats and jugglers and
The laughter of summer in his eyes.

His calligraphy sings swiftly in the air as his hands trace
The characters for JOY, for LIFE and the one for the
HEART THAT IS OPEN.

In the afternoon his brush will elicit dreams, trigrams and
Ancient wisdom from the papers to be spread out in front
Of all of us.

Having learned from teachers we have both been fortunate
To have known, there are moments when we realize
It is perfectly all right to sit and do nothing or to dance.

The sun rises and sets, starlight crosses huge distances;
We have each traveled the four directions and we meet
Once again as if we had never left each other's
Company—my own self with a barrel of hindsight,
Regrets & an eye to the future, my Chinese brother
Teaching the world to dance with ancient wisdom and
Elegant discoveries. The Blue Mountains of Taos look
Over us as we greet each other, pleased with the
Fortune that permits us to meet once again in the fullness
Of summer.

The rustle of the wind in the grass,
The whir of a bird's wings
The sound of the sun,
The cicada at evening—
All these discoveries!

Notes For The Musicians

—for Chen Zhongsen and for his Rose

She plays the Chinese lute, the pi-pah
He plays the two-stringed violin, the erh-hu
Like fisher people they cast their music
Over us, like nets, and draw us in—
They draw us into their boats and smile.

She plays the Chinese lute, the pi-pah
quietly at first, then suddenly, becomes
A summer storm with wind, thunder
And lightning in he hands. Court ladies
Painted on silk scrolls were never like that.

He plays the two-stringed violin, the erh-hu
Lovingly, as one plays with a cat, teasing
The music togo here, to go there,
Up into a tree, out into the sky, back home
Reminding us all of sorrows and delights.

They play their lives together, like spirits
Flying from their sacred mountains to ours
Suddenly appearing, as in the movies, and
Just as quickly to be gone, planting memories
Into our eyes and ears for us to play with.

A Use For Music

—for Stewart Robertson

The making of music by a small orchestra is an
Analog of hope—an idea about which one could
Construct an ordered heaven, understand the
Constellatios and invent logic once again.

Musicians who respect their instruments, their
Art and their ways of being with each other
Understand the mysteries and touch the absolute
With sure hands that know the differences
Between the notes, between the clouds
And between the colors of the rain.

The healing of the music that is made by a
Small group of dedicated players is equivalent to
The laying on of hands by shamans or by
Saints or even by those who have lately
Healed themselves.

Listening to Vivaldi or to Messaien I think of
Wounded friends I would hurry out to find,
To use the music to fix their wounds, to make
Them whole again; to take away the hurt and
Have the sun shine as if it were the first day in
The world.

V. IN THE WORLD

About Agreements

Looking back, looking down the mountain side
It's all about agreements—there they are
All down in the fields, the valleys, the foothills,
All the agreements of your life, scattered —
There, there and there—those that were
Kept and those that were not—those that
Cost and those that were like presents
Discovered, sometimes by accident but more
Often by desire—also all those agreed to
Agreements that were full of reservations,
Those hold backs that made emptiness
Happen and those others made in good faith
That ended up betraying themselves.

Down there, in the litter, yes, there, also
The agreements we made with ourselves,
And then changed. The agreements we
Made with the universe, with the beloved
Of the moment, the beloved for always,
More in hope than anything else

                              and

Then all those others, the ones where we lived
Up to the commitment and the others left
Us hanging, the ones we'd rather forget
And the ones we never will forget
Until that day comes when we check out
Whether we agree on the day and the
Hour or not, it still remains a vista
Of agreements whose colors
Are myriad and whose sense is mostly
Unknown, misunderstood, well meant
And even, in many cases, surprisingly
The way it should have been—
Looking back.

Money

What does this mean, this money, medium of exchange, barter
        quantified, promise to pay?
What is it that rushes us to work for it, dream of it, play or sweat
        for it?
Is it the idea that it manifests? Is it a measure of price, of value or of
        time itself?

Look at what we've done for it! Worked, yes, and long hours and
        conditions as tough as they come until some others sensing that
        something was wrong, unbalanced, not fair, did something
        about it. Talking union.

Look at all the immigrants—and they had to come from somewhere,
        didn't they? so they were emigrants first. Thinking Diaspora,
        Expulsion, New World, Empire. Trade Talks.

Look at the first letters of credit, money in another form, not bullion,
        not pounds and ounces of metal, not sterling but the idea of that
        which would make the exchange worth while. Bankers.

And then over here, see the coins, easy to carry/store/move/take/steal
        each one with an image, at least in the West. In China the original
        marks were only words, ideas. Authority.

Wampum, slaves, cowrie shells, cocoa beans, deeds, indentures,
        dowries, bride prices and the earth in its many forms have been
        indicators in the past; today those concepts all appear as symbols
        on a screen. Transformation.

Now the manifestations in plastic—as powerful as the signet rings of
        other times—electronic fulfillment, immediate gratification,
        balancing resources and abilities. Commerce.

And yes; the markets, farmers and metals and stock markets; thieves
markets and fish markets all dependent on the means of making
this trade, purchase, sale of everything from apples to pearls.
Profits.

Even the tools of the dead, who, by the making of wills, control the future,
the lives of their children's children, even the lives of
nations yet to be formed, in hope or in glory. Power.

Without it starvation, fratricide, love lost and betrayed, children
abandoned, futures pledged for generations of poverty, rags,
bones, heads bowed, homelessness. Poverty.

Collected for good causes by good people in good faith to save souls,
care for the careless; with earthly treasures amassed in the name of
the Spirit. Badges of Devotion. St. Francis.

This money we handle and use every day in one way or another as
part of our lives, as part of our being, begs its own question. Is it
like air that doesn't get mentioned unless it turns foul? Or is it like
light without which nothing grows? This money.

Armies and navies are built with it, wars made with it, not only
between countries but even in the homes and the bedrooms of the
rich and poor who lie for it, dance and sing and sweat for it too.
Hope and Trust.

When there's a lot of it around in any of its forms, particularly when
managed or put away by others, it's not good form to mention it,
talk about it or carry on discussions about it. Done is done.

It's all there, in your hands, in your power to take, to give, to earn and
to die for this thing we call money this quantified power, this
essential harmonic, facilitator and essence of lives too many to
count. Money.

How Far Can You See Today?

The homeless one's horizon is the need
To find the next meal, bed or piece
Of rest before the night falls and worse.

The field hand's horizon is broader,
Knowing the seasons and the work
Will keep him clothed and fed.

The owner and his banker have
A far wider reach. Their eyes
Can see across seas and continents
And consequently are free to plan
Trips to Bali or Antarctica as
Easily as some do to a movie.

There are also those whose
Perch up on that ladder is so
High that they can see clearly
Into the future, making plans for
Their children's children's education,
Place and position in the world.

And then there are those others, who
Climb mountains for the view and yet
Others who like it where they are,
Inventing ceremonies to bless
Their visions and to make them well
While looking inward to their hearts.

An Explanation

The really hard one is to continue
To believe after so many failures,
So many disappointments, so many
Strikes and so much hope gone
Sideways that the bin gets empty
And the spirit's drained.

                    Parables
Of persistence are invoked daily;
Clarifying contrasts are found to
Validate the continuity of effort
And somehow, somewhere, a cache
Of energy is found and one goes
Once more into the negotiation,
Smoothing out the differences,
Once more into the dance, the ritual
That will finally validate the plan
And justify all that went before.

We are all born with persistence in
Our makeup. It's in our blood
And bone—and without it not one
Of us would have learned to walk
Or run or even jump so high that
There are times we can, in fact, go
Up and out and even touch the stars.

Caught Once Again

While caught once again by the story, the homecoming
Of Ulysses, the blood streaming down the halls, Penelope
Surprised and validated—so many questions crowded in—
"Why had I not learned Greek as my sister had?"
"Was it not in Greek that God, the Creator, is known as
"Poet of Heaven and of Earth?" and, *"How old was*
"Ulysses when he returned to bed his wife again?"
And, *"How long had his father managed to live,*
"Tending his garden, surprised his son had come back at all?"
And, *"Why was THEROS the word for Harvest in Greek*
"While no equivalent had made it into Latin?"

                                      The swarm
Of questions buzzing like the summer's bees have
Answers that have no use at all today—questions whose
Burden is inconsequential—and yet without them and
Without those answers you and I are both diminished.

The meadow lark still sings to the setting sun and
Coyote and her pups howl at the moon at night
Without benefit of history or any other lore.

Here the river runs along the meadow's flank
While the mares and foals also run down there.
Here I keep trying to weave Past into Present
And Present into Future while realizing
That today one does not, like Ulysses, truly
Come home again and that the swords
Have not been turned into other things,
While Los Alamos, almost engulfed by fire,
Sits up there on the mountain ready to be let
Loose once more in spite of all the talk of peace.

Statistics

More than ninety-six point nine percent
Of our activities are spent
In various kinds of commerce.

One-half of one percent is spent on love
Including its janissaries and accoutrements.
Point two percent is spent on running,
On often simply sweat.
One whole percent is spent on dreaming
In all its forms

Three and one-half-tenths of one percent
Are spent doing good;
Feeding others, for example,
Others not related by blood, guilt or marriage;
Or burying those unable to bury themselves.

Two and one-half-tenths of one percent
Of all our time is spent on praying—
Some call it reaching out.

The remaining eight-tenths are dedicated
To that rare thing called "doing nothing"
Without which nothing does,
In fact, get done.

Distances

Distance has no meaning until it's measured.
A mile may be considered near or far
Depending on whether one is aboard
A sailing ship or swimming in the sea.

The space we need between ourselves
At a business meeting would seem distant
When occupied by lovers who had not
Been together for a while.
                              We measure
Distances in space as well as time. Feelings
Also are a measure that can be sensed
In terms of distance.
                        How long does it take
For light to move from Betelgeuse to my
Sweeheart's eye and how distant are we
Form the softness of our dreams?
                                    Napoleon
Decreed the distance covered by a meter and
That meter sits today not far from the tomb
In which his bones now rest.
                              The British
Empire, some say, was won or earned
Because a carpenter named Harrison had
Found a way to make a chronometer
That told true time aboard ships at sea
Thereby making possible the measurement of
Distance in ways that are still true today.

There are times I wonder whether we will
Ever find ways to measure the distances
Between the various separate and
Unconnected portions of our lives.

No Excuses

In other times, say, those of Beowulf, or even Caesar's,
There was little room for waffling—your word
Was all there was to rely upon—a quick death
Would be the price of lies, even a mis-statement.
No room then for the excuses that have come
To be the usual language of transactions.
                                      We,
All of us, have become inured to promises unkept,
Terms changed and "Ok, yes, that was the rate
"Last month, last year, but now, it's another thing."
And no recourse.
                     The more civilized and considerate
The climate the more temptation rises to heights
Of irresponsibility.
                       But, one does not have to go
As far back as to the times of Grendel or to
Anthony's disastrous choices to know that we have
Since conspired to build barriers of irresponsibility,
Distributing blame in ways that leave none
Blameless, in a conspiracy of shrugged shoulders
And disappointments.
                     Assassins hide behind
The shields of corporations and no one rises
To accuse the ones responsible for the spread
Of AIDS, of cancers and of the poisoned air.

This planet deserves better manners than those
Evidenced by the current crop of Politicians,
Admirals, Generals & CEO's & CFO's and
Teachers, and Bureaucrats in whose very caring
Hands we have managed to bring ourselves.

Profit accruing to shareholders is not enough
Of an excuse for savaging the common good.

The Practice Of Sacrifice

—for a friend on the occasion
of her double mastectomy

At Delphi they would bring myrtle and oranges
And sweets and clay and silver offerings giving
Thanks for their futures. At Eleusis they would
Bring their questions and their hopes and dreams
As well as olive branches and cattle for the
Priestesses. At Carthage, in the temples, they
Would even bring their first born and snuff them
And leave them in little jars and boxes.

In Tenochtitlan, at the altars on the pyramids, the
Priests would tear out the hearts of prisoners in the
Name of flowers. In the Andes they would
Crush the skulls of young girls dressed for the
Occasion leaving their bodies with offerings in the
Mountain ice. In Spain the pyres of the Inquisition
Charred enough bodies and spirit to merit many
Interesting chapters in the Book of Religions.
In Salem, Mass., they burned witches as sacrifices
For the good of the Commonwealth. In Vietnam
54,000 of ours and millions of theirs were sacrificed
To a vision as stupid as there ever has been, not to
Mention the Holocaust and the Gulag and the Tai
Ping rebellion and all those killed for reasons of color.
Or the Big One, that of Christ, done first on Calvary
And still now, daily, again and again, all over the world.

While today, in America, the breasts of old and
Young women, of beautiful and plain ones, of rich
And poor ones are cut off daily to save their lives,
Their images and their marriages without even a prayer
Or incense on the altar to justify the practice of sacrifice
To stave Death off once again.

Moving From Tesuque

Uproot, deracinate, relocate, start over,
Cast off—all those words indicate
Change, mobility, moving on once more,
Making camp for one night or for a few.

How sedentary we've become !

Surely strange when all our pasts
Were all essentially nomadic.

The society works toward stability
Seducing even the wanderer by
Making it easier to stay than to go.

We've become creatures of comforts,
Attached to the trees we've planted,
To the sunsets we've seen move
From there to there as seasons
Came and went, praying constantly
For the right of staying in that
One place called home and now,
Having to go on once more,
I am reminded that wandering
Is our fate and that permanence
Is delusion.

So long as we have
Feet and eyes and hopes to move us
We go before the long night comes.

New Pesach Poem

Waking slowly that morning the Old
Wanderer, buried in comfort,
Knows this to be the day to move on.

Circe, beautiful, proud and powerful;
Her lands and horses all that any man
In his right senses could possibly want,
Is away.

Then
The reality of the road bit him
And, picking up his staff,
With joints not as operative
As before, taking only that which
He can carry, he leaves.

His head
Knows he has to be beyond the palisade.

Wonders waiting to be fed by him are
Eager and if he were to wait for
Confirmation of the resting places of the yet
To be discovered future, with vouchers,
Tickets and all the rest he would not
Go.

Invoking the memory of Moses he leaves,
Knowing deserts to be there
And dangers in them.
He knows this day
He must be out of Egypt.

Lack of
Attachment, the only safety on the path.

The Two Opera Singers—1943

Almost at the foot of the hills of San Marino, near Rimini,
Where they had heard there might be a place of refuge,
Before dawn, headed south, he, carrying a suitcase,
She with a bundle of clothes, were found walking
Alongside the road by a patrol, brought in, no papers,
Interrogated, then he was made to drop his pants and
"Ach, Juden" the sergeant says, and then,
"Not peasants, look at their hands."

                                They were put on a train,
Going north. They held each other until they arrived at a siding.
There, she was put with the women.

                                A week later he heard her
Voice, singing, Mimi's last aria, across the fence.

He answered as Rodolfo had, repeating his song again
And over again. When the guards told him to stop,
He did not and they shot him.

Lot's Wife

She loved the place they had built together, having
      settled in after Egypt,
After Canaan and after Bethel to find the land rich
      where their daughters had grown.
She had left her heart there when the Lord had
      come down to tell them to pack up
And go, again, from there into the desert to be s
      saved. But she had been happy there,
Quiet, with her heart only in the house and not
      in all that stuff in Sodom.
But it had been the command of JHVH, the Lord ,
      that they leave it all behind
And not look back; but she could not help herself,
      she did turn, and as she did,
She suddenly felt cold—strange how the bitterness
      rose up in her throat.

Quandary

Words change. Their burden depends on who
Says what, and how. "Sorry" can mean regret.
It can also mean insult when flung back to the
Speaker with a question added to it. It's the tone
That makes the music music.

I cannot quote the Father's Tale of Beowulf to
My friend whose son has just been condemned to
Life for murder, knowing he is still convinced of
His son's innocence. The process is not over and it is
His son, and he'll take it to the wall and then
Beyond while I ask myself what I would think
Of doing if I were in his unfortunate and
Weary shoes.

                    I know he must keen and
Weep for his son's life, for the slain unfortunate
Woman found dead in his son's truck, for the
Circumstances that led him, his son, the woman,
The prosecutors and the judge and jury to become
One in this tangle of unhappy circumstance and
Pain and hurt that drops like a stone into the still
Water of our village here, sending ripples out in
This grey October that has forgotten the vari-
Colored thrust of Spring and works its cold into all
Our bones. The sins of sons bounce back to roost
On each and every father's shoulder. *What could
"Ever have been done that was not done?"* Is always
Asked. The ravens wheel and caw against the
White hillside of this early winter afternoon as I
Stare out into the cold not knowing how to say
"Regret" and *"Sorry"* and all those other words that
Should be signals from my heart to a man who is
Both my neighbor and my friend.

Sacred And Profane

—for Page Allen

Are they two houses built next to each other with lawns
        and driveways between them?
Are they two rivers flowing down the mountain from
        adjacent but separate springs with one going one
        way and one the other?
Or are they the two banks of one of those rivers? Or the
        opposite shores of the same ocean?

Was not Lucifer made of the same stuff out of which
        Gabriel and Michael and Rafael and Uriel
        were made?
And when Gabriel came to announce to Mary that since
        she was full of grace she would be from that
        moment on the Mother of God and Immaculate,
        was she not blessed?
And was not Beatrice, who was to sit forever in Dante's
        Heaven the blood cousin of Francesca da Rimini,
        forever damned?

Did not Jesus hang out with thieves and harlots and the
        unclean, while on the way to the Garden
        of Gethesmane?
And in whose house did Mohammed hear the Lord?
Was it not that older, rich woman's house, the one
        belonging to her who had taken him in?
And tell me is it not true that great King David lusted
        after Bathsheba and had her husband dead before
        lunch so that he could have her for his sole self?

The tongue that sings the praises of Emmanuel is often
        the same one that tastes that which is forbidden.
The continuum is there, in ocean aspiring to be cloud, to
        fall again as rain, and so to endlessly sustain.
And where do we turn to find the balance? And is it
        balance that we want or need?

Is it only the Self that shines through, the burning mist of
        geysers bursting out of Earth?

Is it the human spirit that sings while questioning?
Is it the gentleness in human eyes that brings all things
        to a point of peace?
Is the reminder of the rainbow that all colors are one
        and are all children of the Light?

We all wander through patriarchal deserts erecting monuments
        of stone, great walls , pyramids, bell towers and minarets
        to pierce and mark the skies
While we forget that it is the water and wind and dawn and noon
        and dusk and air that are the nurturing and the permanence.
The eyes and lips of the Oracle at Delphi provided sustenance
        to Spirit; the forgotten rituals of Eleusis enhanced
        possibilities for all who came to pray, and it is

The hope of Heaven that moves each hand that rocks a child
        to sleep as the prayers to the Madonna, to Tonantzin,
        Ishtar and to Great Athena, are all sacred and all profane
Joined in the great promise that we will be one with the stars
        when we touch each other, become part and parcel
        of each other as we are star stuff ourselves
And worthy of it ourselves, who are all profane and all sacred,
        all fire and all rain.

La Buena Gente

—for Lu and Mauro

Overcast, this grey day in Spring etches
The calligraphies of cottonwood and locust
Against the cold sky.
                              The sharp wind
Drives the season's expected gentleness
Into the ground.
                              A strange Easter time
This one, when Good Friday brought death
Not only to the One crucified but also to
Ricky and Karen, young lovers killed at
Dawn on their pilgrimage to the Santuario
At Chimayo to celebrate the Resurrection.

Then my sister's husband, like them,
With no warning, falls dead a few
Days after.
                              Illusions of certainty!

The fragility of all our lives confirmed again!

Did Christ know, when the spear pierced
His side He would rise again?
                              The very
First purple and yellow iris, blossoming early,
Flail about in this cold wind, knowing
That even if their petals be shredded
Their kin will be smiling at the sun tomorrow.

When the good ones go like that it is
Belief and trust that are required
To make the Sun return and shine
Again into the trees and flowers and
Into our hearts so that we may
Believe that Spring will indeed return
And that we will continue to know
And praise the good ones who have gone
Before us and before their time.

Machu Picchu

The guide kept telling us how well the stones
Had been cut to fit into each other—one hand's
Fingers fitting around the other hand—there
Was no room to let anything slide in between—
Dark basalt—sheer granite cliffs caressed by
Light clouds with holes in them—distances and
Declivities, opportunities for vertigo that
History alone could not excuse—and the
Gesture once again, this time with hands raised
Above her head, almost the winner's gesture—
As we heard again how the huge rocks had been
Cut and fitted close—and nothing could ever
Penetrate those joinings—then we turned the
Corner—and in the middle of the green of the
Grass, in front of the gray-white clouds drifting
In the center of the wall of dark gray perfectly
Fitted stones, the red flower, Heart of Hope,
Pleasure of Lovers, Carrier Of the Seed of
Tomorrow, Andean Begonia brilliant that
Morning promising more than history, more
Than pleasure growing out of the impossible
Non-existent crevice where the stones had once
Again been fitted and where the impossible had
Been made manifest once again, where the
Heart of the world had been brought out to be
Seen in the red petals that morning in
November in that mountain light.

About Gender

You actor director strong man manager of many
Things writer of stories rider of horses friend
Daring fighter ready to risk all when called upon
Or moved to do so I heard you again this
Morning ask five women how they thought how
They were different from men how they got to
Be where they were how they were different not
One of them said try it from the inside become
One of us learn to love not as part of an
Equation find your way slowly to be quick when
Called upon flow slowly to become water to
Understand why the snakes were driven out of
Ireland men do not find snakes easy to be with
Do not have much room for mystery learn night
Talk give up having the last word learn to serve
Not service try silence for days go inside to find
The place we all come from and be there in the
Dark and breathe slowly and should you ask
Again you will not answer—you will have
Become one of us—

VI. US

Us

We're not many, counting all of us,
Scattered from here to London and
Down to Sydney too, tied loosely,
More or less connected by fate and
Phones and by having done all the
Things we did together while sharing
Memories, appropriating myths and
Then going on to manufacture
Our own interpretations
Of being alive.
                    Tribal and familial
On one side while wholly singular on
The other, we choose to shape our lives
So as to be involved with those with whom
We share our dreams and dances,
Our bread, our peaches, our thoughts
And our histories.
                    One day the children's
Children will say "Oh yes, we know,
"They came from over there, and then
"Were here for a while before they
"Went on" — all the data to be
Stored in computer memories so as
To be accessible in ways undreamed
Before today.
                    Every thing that was
Before is here. Touch it. It's us now
And will be them in time.

Epithalamion

*—for Rachel and Todd on the occasion of
their wedding day in May 1998*

A gathering of all that went on before
A bringing in of lives and dreams and dances,
Of music, hopes and happenstance,
Of tears and hurts and mending and
Of smiles, clouds and all remembering.

A basketful of new beginnings, grateful for
All that went before, thankful that
All our varied roads all led to this one day
Of joy to mark a shining time
In your calendar of being and of life.

The world that you have made together
Is one that shines for all of us, joined
As we are, in loving you, reaffirming
Once again that love confirmed is
Reaffirmed in ways that shape the world.

Skylarks turning cartwheels in the air in Spring,
Hummingbirds that make the wind stand still
And the lilacs and the iris all do it without
Mistake—Learn from them and not from us
How to invent the loves that last and last.

Shining with one light from this day on
While maintaining each your separate strengths
You have joined your willingness to trust and
To be each other's joy—You have our hearts,
Keep them safe with yours for happiness

And you will, you will, be well!

Pranha

—*For Debora and Scot*

"Breath of my breath," she said.
"Life of my life," he said.
Star stream, angel fire and
So many dangers overcome
By the two of them before
They could find each other
And themselves in each other's
Arms, eyes, hearts and hopes.

"Breath of my breath," he said.
"Life of my life," she said.
Now fields of alfalfa stretch
From the old house down
To the river and all the past
Is ground to the future flowering
Of their lives in each other's
Arms, eyes, hearts and hopes.

"Heart of my heart," he said.
"For always my love," she said.

A Friend Sends A Poem

—for Manly Johnson

Time stretches its horizons to encompass new friends
And to make them as precious as the old ones. One
Twenty minute sojourn in a man's house tells you
More than twenty years of encounters at the bank
Or in the marketplace or at a party in some
Club or stranger's place.

        And then, when of a
Sudden, in an unexpected afternoon full of gray November
That new friend sends a shaft of out of season
Summer sunlight full of apricots and appreciation
The day itself turns into a recognition that mirrors
Pleasures given and pleasures received, in a poem,
Becoming a flower, a piece of evensong or even that
Rattle of castanets that wakes one up to think
That yes, it's all right, it is in fact worth more
Than the ruminant pursuit of busy ness
That cloaks old habits.

        How good that friendship still
Can sing and turn its brightness onto every thing!

For My Sister And My Brothers

Our father thought that Abraham
Had been more than one person in his time,
The name Ivrim having been given to
The border crossers, river jumpers
And all those who had crossed over
Gotten away, made it out and
Made it to the other side of Jordan,
Or of Ocean or other frontiers.

Ivrim, plural of Ivri, in Arabic
Becomes Ebrim, Abram,
And then Abraham. The one
Who fathered all of us.
                               Our mother
Loved him, and like Ruth, not only followed
But, with unexpected strengths, made
A new world brave and possible
For all of us.
                       They loved each other
Until the end, each in his own way,
Not only as lovers but as friends.

Once people reach into each other's hearts
And find the secret of each other's lives
They change and become each other
In ways that any one outside will
Find difficult to discover.
                               We are
Each one of us, made up of the two
Of them and each breath we draw
Is drawn because of their love
For each other and for us. We are
Alive because of them and this world
Exists for us only because of them.

A Birthday Sonatina For Mark

The grey cement, turgid, lumping heavily, falls and pours out of
The rolling vat into the trench, makes itself into a footing, a
Foundation, to become a base of structures as light as the birds
Of summer, as brilliant as macaws and bluejays, structures
Manifesting spirit in steel, soul in the body of the world.

Your inventions sing out with joy, with the exuberance that
Pounces catlike out of the dark, out of the difficult places, to
Stride bravely once more over mountains, across oceans,
Establishing colonies, beachheads and playgrounds for children
Of all ages and places.

Your inventions give the lie to the fashions of one week or the
Other, are the measures by which others are measured while you
Continue to dream of dolphins, of frigate birds and of dragons
Dancing in the breezes of China.

Your inventions are beacons in all kinds of weather, marking the
Confines of safe and good places, answering questions no one
Has asked with answers made up of laughter, of the structure of
Numbers and of the ways of the world.

Your inventions are parables in the language of vision that move
The viewer into the spaces beyond, the ones where the heart
Sings, engaged and committed.

Now, the Great Wheel of Time turns Summer into Fall with its
Colors and blessings, while I dream of you easing up on the
Throttle, double clutching down on the gearshift, bringing the
Long arm of the crane into boomrest, into harvest and honey,
Knowing how well you have done and how hard it has been for
You while swinging on scaffolds and reinventing the lever,
Knowing it always begins with that slurpy cement pouring out
Of the vat to become the foundation for the tracing of light, which
Is live.

For Henry In The Austral Sea

It still appears to be at the end of the world, this
Place of deserts surrounded by water, discovered
By you, all those years ago when our place of refuge
Became a place of pain for you.
                                              You bravely
Confronted distances again, on your own
To make your own world unentangled by all
That had gone before, brining protection
To the indefensible as you have always done,
Merging your sense of justice with that which
Is written, moving from church to temple and
From whirling dervish ecstasy to the contemplation
Of that which is, you now move beyond the pale,
The palisade to reach into infinity.

                                              All the duties
Behind you, the border and ocean crossings with
The Sepic your Jordan and Ayer's Rock
Your Sinai; you move into the wilderness at
The edge, always and again at the edge, of sea, of
Memory, of presence, of community, of families,
Creating your own version of all that was before,
In all the other continents you've known,
Always on the way, becoming, overcoming.

Forerunner and vanguard, we all are
Indebted. You, reminding all of us that
The other is always wherever you are
Breathing and sleeping, growing, becoming,
Running and eating, and loving in time.

Post Op

I.

He wakes in a room full of walls
With the ceiling threatening to come
Down.

   He wonders that he is there at all,
Touching the edge of the sheet with
Surprise. The last thing he remembers
Was trying desperately to claw his way
Out of a dark blood red curtained room
Towards the exit that would take him out
Away from his life and all its complications
On the other side of that room.

Striated sinew walls, dark, very
Dark blood red with no light at all
With the screech of a metal saw
Coming through those curtains, heavy
Like wet meat, dark red and so,
Evidently, they—whoever they were —
Doctors and nurses, anesthetist,
All together, managed to stop him,
To make him turn back and not go
Through that wall of blood but
Instead turned him around
And pulled him back towards
The light, the air, his life to
Wake in a room full of walls
That were beige and quiet
And not pulsing but plain,
With even the ceiling
Steadying itself and staying
Up there where it belonged.

II.

Once upon a time he wondered
Whether somewhere there was
A saint whose name no one
Knew, a patron saint of the
Near miss and close call. He
Remembered asking that saint
His name and forgot about
The event since the saint
Had not answered.

            After
This most recent close call of
His he thought again
Of that saint who had not
Answered. Knowing now
He owed him another
Near miss, another close call.
His name did not matter much
At all, though he knew
That he owed him all.

                He went
Out into the hills and he
Gathered dead falls of piñon
And juniper and made a very
Small fire whose smoke went
Up to the clear blue sky slowly
Carrying his thanks once more
To that saint of the near miss,
The one of the close call.

III.

He went out, back into the world
The one he had almost left for good
And began to pick up the pieces
Of a life he had almost lost —
Looking at them as if they had been
Pieces of a jigsaw puzzle he
And the family would piece
Together during the holidays —
A puzzle with which he was
Familiar—like an almost
But not quite remembered
Old novel written by some
Acquaintance of his whose
Name did not quite come
To him—and then, yes, he
Began to recognize the many
Characters, the roles they
Were playing, the feelings
They expressed for him. It
All seemed strange to him
For a while but soon he
Came to realize this really
Was his life and no one
Else could play it out for
Him and he just would
Have to finish it on his own.

Waves

—*for Alexander*

They have their sequences, reasons to come
And beat their greetings on the shore, regularly
At times, at others with a rhythm sprung
From the deep of ocean and then as if to make a
Point, a cluster, waves crowning in on each other,
Demanding attention, storm roaring now, gentle
Lapping later and each one different, much as we
Humans are with each other, with moods
Dependent on wind, weather, an occultation of the
Moon, or even the imponderable effect of chance.

And if one is fortunate enough to have learned how
To catch one, how to balance and how to ride it
Into shore, smiling, one could then expect to use
That way of doing things even when no longer at
The beach.

Waking, then, with gentle help, healing, discovering
I had come back I thought how silly Lazarus must
Have felt coming back after the funerary feast had
All been finished and cleaned up and I was as
Surprised as anyone who gets that close to the edge
And manages to come back.

All the pieces did begin to fit back together; the
Christmas jigsaw puzzle was at hand, and the
Involvement in a cousin's marriage a continent away,
With medieval complications along the side
All managed to work together to bring me back.

I soon found myself at work, adding, subtracting
And dividing as if nothing had happened to me or
To change my world, and yet it seemed

The seasons chased each other the way carriages in
A train do when the rails are in the mountains
And—not knowing the specifics of the journey—I
Took my seat, looked out at the incomparable view,
Wondering still how I had made it through the
Waves, up to the beach and then further up to the
Mountains on a train with my destination still
Unclarified while summer's forests bring their green
Graces up to be with very white white clouds in
The mountain air so clear and blue the sky evokes
The sea again. The waves, the waves, the waves,
The waves.

The Same and Not The Same

Brow creases, recognition comes,
But a bit more slowly now.
Yes, you do remember, and who
Was it who first built the Jeep?
You know—Willys—and
You do remember and you're pleased
When you remember it's Bill
Coming down the sidewalk, but
You're not absolutely sure so
You say, "Hi there" and smile
And let it go at that—

                    But
You do remember that high jump
At your first track meet when
You were twelve and the bite
Of the sawdust when you came
Down into it knowing you had
In fact sailed up and over
And the wind tasted of smoke.

One Year After

The Surgeon

"Fine", he said *"just fine"* you've been doing well—
"It's been a year and, frankly, there aren't
"That many that pull through as well as you have—

"Complications, you know, and you were 100 cc's
"Away from the morgue, old boy, you know you
"Had a lot of luck going because, even when we
"Do our best we never really know."

    And I thanked him again and thanked
His two fellow surgeons wondering
What it was, really, that had done
The Job, pulled me through, so that
I could wake clear-headed and bright
On a Summer's day dealing with all
The various pieces of my life as if
I had not skidded to the edge so
Close, that, on coming back, each leaf
On every tree, each rock along the road,
Each truck, each car, each person in
My life seemed brighter than before.

The Doctor

"Yes, they did the cutting and the patching and
"The sewing it back up so that it works—
"But you know it was the holistic stuff
"That pulled you through—nature that made you
"Well."

       She said, and I, thankful that all had
Worked together, in a conspiracy of fixing
What had gone wrong bowed and promised
To take care.

The Daughter

"Dad, you know it wasn't time for you
"To go—look at all there is to do, here
"And everywhere."

No doubt at all in a child's eye.

The Friend

"So wonderful to see you so fit after all
"You went through, please take care."
And then he went on to say that, No
One at all could do it for me, as if I
Had not heard that one before.

My job still not complete. The work
Not done yet and the demands of
Warmth and growth and the use of
Water in the fields all there once again
To make sure that there is still a laugh
Or two to be shared, humor and delight,
Amusement and amazement all part
Of our own process, as we go on trying
To make sure the harvest will in fact
Be there for all of us.

In the March 1999 issue of the Atlantic Monthly, David M. Kennedy, Professor of History at Stanford University presented an article entitled "Victory at Sea." It speaks of "the sweep and strategic stakes of the war at sea in which 104,985 American sailors and Marines were wounded, 56,683 were killed and more than 500 U.S. Naval vessels were sunk. Lest we forget." Professor Kennedy' properly employs the historian's overview accurately reporting data and the facts without touching on the human elements of those memorable events. The feelings and sacrifices and the personal specifics of those days are not mentioned., nor is there any mention at all of the significant supporting role played by the men and ships of the U.S. Merchant Marine, without whose involvement there would have been no Victory at all. I know of no official tally of the casualties among the Merchant Mariners, nor do I have a count of those other ships that went down alongside the U.S. Navy's ships — but — having sailed as an able bodied seaman on deck on ships that performed a portion of the supply function required for all the Victories in the Pacific, from the Russell Islands to New Guinea and the Philippines I saw and experienced aspects of those days unnoticed by Professor Kennedy. My reaction to the impersonality of his overview triggered the development of a song cycle whose view is from below, not from above and whose intent is to flesh out the story in human terms. A selection of the songs written up to this point in time follows.

——*Victor di Suvero*

VII. SEA SONGS

A Selection From
Sea Songs—

—for my Father, for Jim San Jule
and for all the men I sailed
with in those days.

.First Set

First Song

I sing of the arms of the men who carried,
Who hauled, stowed, shoved, nailed and tied
Those cargoes that made that victory at sea
Possible, that made it possible for the work
To be done before the ships even went to sea, all
Those men whose hands measured the steel
Before it was cut into the shapes that made
The hulls that would be launched to take
The places of the ones sunk in the Atlantic,
Destroyed in the Pacific and drawn ashore
On the reefs of unnamed islands from
The Aleutians to Antarctica and driven
Down into the deep by storm and gunfire.

I sing of the arms
Of those who had honed their skills on
Steam schooners, hauling lumber from Coos Bay
And Gray's Harbor down to the mills in
Oakland, on fishing boats whose home ports
Were well hidden behind glaciers in Alaska,
On oil tankers steaming their flammable cargoes
Out of Richmond and San Pedro out to Hawaii
While their brothers on shore fought the shape up,
The longshore bosses and the ship owners.

I sing of those arms that were strong enough
To dance the drums of lube and other oils
Across steel decks down in the holds of ships
And of those other arms made mostly of bone,

Of the young ones, who had more will than sense,
Who had gone down to the sea before their beards
Had grown into beards, because they wanted to help.

I sing for the voiceless, for all those drowned —
For all the others who found their deaths on
And above the sea's surface, were buried there
In that great silence, the great cold, until their flesh,
Their blood and their bones became once
Again part of that salt sea from which we all came.

I leave it to all those others, statisticians and
Historians, all those numerologists who write
And publish the details of battles listing
The ships that went down at Midway, the subs
That were sunk in the Atlantic with the numbers
Of those that went down with them. My interest
Does not sit in counting how this admiral
With his flagship and flag had sweated this
Battle turn or that one, and what his hunch
Had done for him, or for us, or rather to us
Out on lookout or down in the engine room
Not knowing, not ever knowing, whether
His choice, his judgment would bring us
Life or bring us death before night fall.

Second Song

I am amazed that more than half a century
Has sloshed through the scuppers and that
No one has taken the time or the interest
To put down, for the children and for
Those that will come after them how it was
Out there where nothing breaks the wind's thrust,
Nothing interrupts dawn light or starlight

For day after night after day after night
While the coffee is made for each watch
And while food is cooked and served and
Sextants are sighted and lifeboats checked
And men go to sleep so close to each other
That one's breath becomes the breath of another
And where one learns to lock dread away
Having no control at all over one's living or dying.
It is those arms and backs, that energy that moved
Those cargoes whose makeup in the holds and
Up on deck became the engines of war. Those B-25s
Lashed down without wings were lifted over the side
By the cables stretched between booms as
The ship anchored out off the beach at
The Russell Islands, north of Guadalcanal,
While the palm trees swayed in the eyes
Of the plow jockeys from Missouri who had
Grown up the week before when the first Zeros
Had strafed the convoy the first time.
That which later was called "strategy,"
And the Orange Plan, dating back to other
Wars and other lives, determined the way
Those arms would reach up to steady the load
As it was winched up and over the side
Down into the lighter to be hauled ashore hoping
No more of those Zeroes would come in to clatter
Their chatter as they went by.

                    There's more
Than one kind of sweat we learned—the sweat
Made by work in the heat and the one
Made by fear—and while sweating both
Kinds, off loading the planes and the gear,
Wondering whether the skipper's aware
How salt those sweats are, out on deck,

In the tropics, at night I could not
But think how it always has been different
For those on the bridge and for
The rest of us down where we were.

Third Song

The push down towards Australia by the Japanese
Brought modern warfare to the sky people in New Guinea.
Those stone age examples of what we had been
And where we're going — down to the coast they came —
Barefoot, curious, muscles rippling, picking cigarette butts
Up with their toes. They came to see us,
White and black, not well made like them, not
As agile; ignorant like walking ghosts who grunted.
They too were recruited to help move the cargo,
To get stores down to the beach where needed
In all those places with strange names, Rabaul,
Finschafen, Hollandia and back to Lae.

Then sailing up to Biak to pick up what was
Left of that battalion of Marines who came aboard
With a five pound sugar sack full of gold, the teeth
They had knocked out of the mouths
Of the enemy that had been killed and then that
First lei of ears around the corporal's neck —
Souvenirs — remembrances — wondering how
They would keep — would they dry like flowers do?
Nothing like that in the official version
Nothing like that when it comes time
To make monuments — nothing in the histories
About the gunner in the gun tub aft letting go
When the first wave of Zeros did come over
With his loose shit making everyone slide
About as the ship keeled and bounced us

Around — no record of the noise — the clatter.
There are all the others who have made
A record of those times on land when,
Locked in battles whose names reverberate,
Armies surged and ploughed into each other.
No one as yet has put down for the sake
Of all those who lived through or who did not
Those watery days where one lived each day
On deck's edge, each day not knowing
If it would be the last while thinking of that girl
Or father or mother or brother while standing
Wheel watch, lookout, or oiling bearings,
Checking stores and doing all the things that
Every ship has always needed once it's launched.

Steel, painted or bloated, beginning to rust
Under the paint, steel wire, cables, oiled,
Ready, hatch covers battened down, ready
To take wind's howl or wave's hit,
Always ready, without ever being sure
What we were ready for — no subs up
Here, but you never know — the bos'un
Barking, the fire drill, boat drill and
Then when the General Alarm screams
The running, stations, muttering, questions,
In place, a few loud sons o'bitches,
The mate shouting, then the silence
Permitting the base drum of the engine
To thud and make the ship's heartbeat
Match your own while the questions
Begin to bubble up — What is it this time?
Where is it? What the fuck is it this time?
Then "all clear" and you stand down
Relieved and furious at the same time
Whether it's ten at night or on the star watch
Back to your bunk and breathing slow.

Fifth Song

All those shipmates, the ones that sang
And from whom I learned about Joe Hill;
Johnny, the Filipino messman, who ran
The poker game, Cookie, the big black
Negro cook who put "hot stuff" in every dish
He cooked for us and dreamt of coming back
Ashore to be a preacher, which he did, and
The Third Assistant Engineer, Ed Brady who
Only thought of skiing while the ship headed
South into the heat of Islands, of Gauguin,
Of Mutinies on Bounties, and all he could
Think about was powder and the girls
That he had tumbled in front of the fire
At the lodge and those pleasures kept him
Going while standing dogwatch, the 12 to 4,
In the engine room noise below while
A thousand like him on all the other ships
Going and coming across the oceans over
And under which the war was being fought
Were living other lives in their heads, while
Dice were being thrown, guesses made, gut
Feelings expressed up there in the ward rooms
That would determine their living or dying;
And it is those shipmates, the ways they
Smelled, they sang, they dealt the cards
And stood their watches that only
Appear in the historical summations
As numbers in the various columns —
Those who survived, those who did not —
Without reference to their relatives, their songs
Or any other human feeling part of them.
And, as I sing of all those who were A-1
And were drafted, of the cream of the crops

Of Indiana, Washington, California and Montana,
Of all the other states where volunteers
Swelled the ranks of those who went to sea
I must also sing of the ones too old
For the draft and the ones too young — those
Who were gimps of one kind or another or
Technically "enemy aliens" even though they
Had managed to find shelter in
The arms of America when hounded
Out of Germany and Italy and Japan
And, as dedicated, if not more, than
The ones who joined up because it was
The right thing, the American thing, I sing them
And I sing Robeson singing the great
Ballad for Americans
Giving voice to an idea whose time
At last had come, making the dream
Tangible, along with Rivera's frescoes
And the Refregier murals in San Francisco,
Defining the good even before the world
Came to know the depths of Dachau and
The stench of all the other camps whose
Viciousness as agencies of death
Still rattle belief and make men
And women and children stare, shake
And choke at the scope and power of evil,
Before Bataan, before the fire storms of Dresden,
Of Tokyo and before Little Boy and Fat Man
And the winds of Nagasaki and Hiroshima.

Sixth Song

It's not that one kind of death really differs
From another—when the spirit leaves, it
Leaves body and thoughts and relatives

119

All behind—bones are bones when buried
In dirt or dragged down to the sea's floor—
And yet the cold mention that there were
Twelve thousand dead in this engagement
And at Leyte, the biggest sea battle of
The war only 3,560 of ours died in those
Three days when each one of us who was
There knew we were less than pawns,
In terms of the big game being played —

Never before did death surf on waves
Of blood so high that the waging of sea
War was forever changed—and after
Those three days of being on deck, after
Only one small bomb hit us on
The fantail, with Corey's arm hanging
Loose down his left side and held only by
Skin and muscle while deciding to
Cut it loose or not, not thinking
About Admirals, only about do we
Get to tomorrow now that the three
Platoons of engineers have been off-loaded
On to the LCVs that appeared in the water
Below us and finally to stand down
After seventy hours of nerves to then
Wake with the General Alarm ringing
And Corey's blood spurting out
With each heart beat again
Once more to tumble out on deck
With dawn breaking and the striated
Clouds catching the sun's pink with
The last stars in the corner, corny
As all get out but there it was
And the shout going from ship to ship
In that great curve of Leyte Bay as

The dots down there became planes
And the twin fuselages told us P-38s,
They were ours and not the buzz saws
Of those Zeroes that had bitten all of us
Again and again as MacArthur got ready
To step ashore out of the landing craft
When he returned and we all heard
Him saying he had returned while we
Started the cleanup, taking deep breaths
Knowing we had come close to the list
Of those that would be remembered
Only as some of the numbers of men
Among those that had died that day
In the Greatest Sea Battle of the war
As it would come to be known.

Seventh Song

Sprague
Had the shakes for a week after Leyte.
Nineteen, called Lefty because his left
Side was just a bit shorter than his right,
Had learned to climb and do about anything
Anyone whose sides were equal could do.
After Leyte he hardly talked any more
He'd just stand there and shake, get
The lines stowed, sweep, hose down the deck,
But then, stand up and shake, going down
Off watch to his bunk, still shaking, then
Got better, stopped shaking—but it
Would come back from time to time.
When he went down the gangway when
We finally made port with seabag
On shoulder, he walked as straight
As he ever had but when his feet

Hit dock he put his seabag down—
Sat on it shaking, and he put his head
Down on his knees and his short left arm
Waving loosely out there in the air,
Shaking, with his pay in his pocket,
Shaking, going to get home somehow
But never to be listed as anyone
Of the casualties of that Great Sea Battle
Of Leyte Bay where today, my son
Tells me a huge new landing strip
Is being built to land 747's at the
Edge of the jungle to serve the tourists
Scheduled to come to a great new
Resort with the capacity of housing
More guests per night than all those
Who died in those three days to secure
The landing of MacArthur and his troops
In those three terrible days worth not
Even a footnote in the histories to come.

Tenth Song

I sing Kohl's arms trying to budge
The steel dogs that had jammed when
The torpedo hit and how he must have
Felt as that salt sea slowly caught him
By the throat — and I know that
Leyte was only one step in the march —
Back to Hollandia — to reload, then
Back north again to Lingayen Gulf
Which somehow seemed easier and
Not as scary as the Leyte bit —
But then that's where I bought
Sinbad, a long tailed monkey, for
A carton of Pall Malls and found

I had bought myself a friend I could
Fuss over, clean up after, worry about
So that the big picture didn't matter
And even when Charley the Carpenter
Had to be taken ashore having drunk
Himself blind on paint thinner strained
Through a loaf of bread — that was
Certainly not a casualty of the war
But of his own stupidity — for which
There is no excuse — and Sinbad
Learned to reeve a line through blocks
Up on the booms and raised hell
Making everybody smile.

Had to put him in a sack and over
The side when we got back to Seattle
With three shackles to take him down
Because otherwise the whole ship
Would have been quarantined and six
Days out at anchor after nine months
At sea would have been enough to
Send us both over the side.
Even Sinbad in the sack
Voiceless, drowning down in Puget Sound
Does not figure in the end.

Twelfth Song

So now I sing
For the voiceless, for those, who
Dreading the moment, stood
Silent at their posts until
It was right for them to move.
Count the dead, yes, but make
Each one of that number come

To life one last time, give him
His name, and tell us where
And how it hurt and the pain
Or the shock before going down
So that the children will know
And, knowing, perhaps choose
To stop the repetition of that
Kind of insanity that kills men
And kills women and children
For no reason but greed
In the name of glory and greatness.
I sing now remembering sunlight on water,

The bow wave, its curl reaching out,
Flying fish dancing, moonshadows,
The slap of cordage on mast, clouds
Racing into weather, the thunk
Of bow dropping in to wave trough,
Anchor chain racing, spray blowing
And night watches that taught me
The shapes of being alone on the sea.

Thirteenth Song

But to go back now, back to all those
That sailed before, back to Ulysses
Back to Jason and the Argonauts, back
To the Vikings who sailed down to raid
As far as Sicily and the coast of Africa,
Back to the dreams of Henry the Navigator,
Of da Gama and Columbus and Magellan,
Of Vespucci, Caboto and Nelson
And even of Byrd and Nobile and Millo —
They all were there then and in our heads today —
Because of their crews, the unnamed and

Unremembered crews — yes — a few lieutenants,
Mates, officers and sailors can be found
If one looks carefully enough — and I know
That the members of the chorus are hardly
Ever known by name but without their voices
No Dies Irae no Te Deum can reach
Into your gut to wrench your spirit
And move your blood.

"On that day," we say, as if we were
At Agincourt or in the Armada, or
Sailing to Noumea or to Iwo as people
Have always said when remembering
The result — our victory, our triumph
Or when we suffered this sinking or
That disaster or that Lepanto —
Depending on which side your father
And your mother belonged to when you
Came out of your own salt sea to light —

And you had no name but sat amidships
And set sail, wind jamming tiller,
With casks of water and supplies, drawn
By your dreams and that beckoning
That draws each sailor away and out
Beyond horizon's line to discover that
Which is always there beyond beyond.

<u>Second Set</u>

First Song

There was hardly a one aboard
That did not have someone
Ashore. Hardly a one without
Mother or brother or daughter

Or son. Hardly a one that
Sailed alone and lived or died
Alone. There were times when
The gooneys, gliding above the wake,
Seemed to be stand-ins for
All the ones ashore, worried
About us when there was nothing,
Nothing to worry about.
                          It would
Or would not happen, St. Christopher
Medals, amulets; Jack Nye had a
Toe ring long before its time, a cord
From a prayer shawl, a locket with
Hair in it, a holy card taped up
On the bulkhead, a lucky penny,
A belt buckle, Ben's father's razor,
All of them counted, not one of
Them counted. It would or
Would not happen.

               And dreams,
Wet ones, dry ones, full of scary
Shit ones, wanting ones and
The curious ones that did not
Go anywhere, have anything
To do with where we were, or
Where we were going all piling
Up into connections with the life
Ashore that had been left behind.

Third Song

But the sea's not changed, the sea
Still moves its tides in concert with the moon
And men still sail upon its waters never

Really knowing what tomorrow's winds will bring,
Confusing hope and certainty, accomplishment
And desire the way that little children will.

I sing these memories to myself when I walk
These hills and valleys that once were parts
Of an ocean floor knowing as little now as
I did then and sure of a lot less while I
Retrace those voyages and prod recollection
So as to dredge up some scraps that could
Yet serve the ones who will still be here
When I am gone.

              Heave away Raio, I'm off
To Venezuela and then I'm heading
For Shanghai!
              I sing for my shipmates,
All those I've sailed with from time to time
From the Golden Gate to Singapore and
From Venice to Tientsin and for
All those without voices, mute
In the sea's roar and silent
In the war's rages of that time before.

'Do yourself a favor," I've been told,
"And forget about it now — you
"Made it through even though
"All those others didn't — the sun
"Is shining and there's a plenty
"In the land — why don't you just
"Forget it the way everyone else
"Already has?"

              Heave away Raio,
Heave away my bonnie boys, we're off

To Venezuela, we're off to see the girls
A dancing on the shore!
                            And then
It comes back again, morning time and
Evening time and out there
In the middle of the nowhere sea
You hear Porgy singing out to Bess
For the very first time, your own
Heart's hurt and you ask
"Who is that?" and "Where
"Did that come from?" and the
Armed Forces Radio Service
Somehow reaches and teaches
And I cannot forget the way
Those things managed to sing
Their way into the times
I remember and sing today.

Seventh Song

So long ago and yesterday
Almost like the Ace of Spades
And the Jack of Hearts, depending
On which one you pick up and
Which one you lay down — they
Can be short, they can be long
An eternity ago, alive today
And this morning's coffee no
Different than the one I drank
The other day.
                        Like an accordion
Played by the hands of fate —
Time's tune can make you smile
And in the next moment, cry. It
Can make you dream and sigh

And make you remember things
Buried and gone so long ago. It
Will draw a note out for so
Long a stretch you know it
Will never end and the days
And nights go by each with its own
Tempo and that boom can take
An hour to fall onto the deck
When it just misses you while
A week ashore can be gone
In only one hour's span —
                                        So
Long ago and yesterday all here
In the storeroom of the heart
That beats in time to keep
The rhythm of the accordion's tune
So that we can all end
Up dancing for a while,
Until it's time.

                        That's why
I sing of the arms of the men
Who did all those things that
Made it possible for the wars
To be fought, the wars to be won,
So that we may end our days
Knowing it was better that it
Turned out the way it did —
And, yes, the Admirals decided
Which way to turn the fleets
And which way to storm,
Which way to fly and each one
Did what had to be done —
But each mother's son
Who was killed or drowned

Or torn apart or crazed
As a result was as much
Part of the song as any other
And whether their names will
End up being remembered or not
Each and every one was worthy
Each and every one was there
And without them and without
Their arms and backs and hands
And eyes and trust there never
Would have been any victory at all
At sea or any other where at all.
And I will continue to sing
So long as breath is left to me
To keep memory alive before
It turns into history
And to celebrate the lives
Of all those who worked
And fought and sang and died
Not listed in the official lists
Unremembered and unsung
But still alive for me.

Ninth Song

To be alone, on lookout, the ship and crew
Behind you, following; to be one with the stars,
With the sense that there is no other,
Anywhere and the rise and fall of the bow,
As regular as breath can be when one's asleep,
The sea, asleep and still alive with light,
The phosphorus breaking out of bow wave,
The thud coming from time to broken time,
Not regular, as discordant as cry of sea gull
Or of memory not quite rhythmic,

Not quite like anything but itself,
Listening to it, bracing against it,
Standing with the cold just beginning to climb
Into your back's bones thinking how dying can come
If it does in fact come, slowly, like that cold on lookout.

Seeing everything and nothing with the ship
And crews abaft with only the universe around you
Knowing it's your sight alone that may save, guard,
Protect all the rest that may or may not be there,
While the bow rises and the bow falls,
Alone.

Twelfth Song

Going ashore, paid off, seabag on your shoulder from
One world to another—the same and not the same—
Gangway leading down to the dock, dry land, home
Port, who's out there, what has changed, is she really
Going to be there?
            Rush of daylight, asphalt, not
Steel decking to stride on, but through the dock's
Dark sheds, out juts the light on the other side.
                            Ashore.
The other world not daring to call it home—yes—
Home port—but home, no not sure, gone only nine
Months—paid the dues, paid Smokey the poker
Game losses, gave Tom what he had coming—now,
Paid in green, walking down, first steps into that
Other parallel world that does not rock—no tide
Moves it and yet keeps changing—newly found.
Ashore.

VII. RIFFS

Riff #1

Sight

Where was I when I woke in that bed
Set against the wall where the saws
And the drills were buzzing their clatter
With their points almost reaching the pillow
I had put my head down on, almost
Reaching my skull, my brain case, full
Of all that which I wanted to keep?
Where was I? I couldn't answer. All
I could do was jump, out of bed, out
Of my skin, almost, and cold outside
And I hit the deck running, barefoot
With the grinding persistence of drill noise
And saw noise carving the wooden wall
Chasing me down the hall until I got
To the street, buck naked, shivering
Wondering why and still dark outside
And no one in the alley or around
The corner, the piazza, the coffee shop
And I ducked back in the door
Before it closed, moused my way back
Up the stairs again, found my room
Reached in for my overcoat and grabbed
As the whole wall behind the bed
Crashed down offering a vista of mountains
I had never seen before, a panoply
Of clarity, of distances, peak after peak,
White and that other color of light, grey
Blue and white again, all stretching out
To the limit of the eye's reach and I still
Did not know where I was or how I had
Gotten there to put my head on that pillow
In that room at the end of that corridor that night.
Where was I when I woke
Up in that bed, where?

Riff #2

Appleman

"Bring me your apples," he cried, standing
On the corner by his press. *"Bring me your apples*
"and I'll squeeze them into juice, ferment them
"into Jack and give you all the warmth of summer
"back again, in a glass, in a jug, in your hand
"before the sun goes down!"

                             This is what he had
Been trained to do -- he could do anything at all
With the apples people brought to him.

                                   A red
Cloak, a yellow hat with a twig coming out of it.
It was said that if you cut him open his flesh
Would be white and sweet, and yes there
Would be hard segments and dark seeds
But all in all rather digestible and very few
Would remember that bad business about the
Snake in the Garden and Eve and Adam
And all that trouble that started
Way back then and how his family
Had learned the trade and passed it on to him
To squeeze apples, to crush them, to offer
To do anything at all with them.

                                   You see
It was his job and as long as he did it well
There would be some balance out there
In the world and people would think of
His kind in a kindlier way given that
He would make juice and Jack for them
And they would not have to remember
The place and reason for their troubles.

"Bring me your apples"
Your apples," he cried.

Riff #3

Heaven

If Heaven were a mall and one could saunter
By the various offerings and be surprised to see
The infinite variety of ever afters that had
Been established in the names of all the Gods
One then could be intelligent about Eternity.

One could satisfy one's quick curiosity about Mohammed's
Version of the vision and, seduced by the
Amplitude of his imagination, loiter in the sensual
Structures erected for the faithful and the brave

Or one could climb the mountains of that chain called
Paradiso to sit upon a peak and bathe in bliss
Before the presence of the Presence recognizing
Beatrice and all the glory of Dante's edifice

Or one could be invited to drink tea in the afternoon
With Shiva practicing on his drum for the concert
With the milkmaids who would always strum
Along and teach the rest of us to be gentle and to be wise.

Or, wanting something a bit more fiery we could
Enter Kali's shop whose skull collection is quite
Sufficient to make you drop your guard and
Chill the summer heat right out of your skin, not
To be confused with the Tibetan connection, down a
Cloud or two, past Olympus, yes, and also past
Calvary, there where all the Black Hats still
Shake their fringe of skulls to show their power.

Now that Management has finally arranged to offer
In and out privileges if one's really been OK it
Certainly makes Eternity a more possible piece of
Time than it's ever been before.

Riff #4

Mysteries

All of them—the pronounceable ones and the other ones—
The ones we live by and the other ones—The ones on which
Belief systems are based—Joan of Arc—led into the fire—
The warrior maiden—Mishac, Shadrach and Abednego—
Led out of the fire. Mysteries we live by—and with—who
Are we, as a race, that we believe things that turn us into
Things less than Wars of the Flowers—Hearts torn out and
Offered as sacrifice to the Sun—always the system of
Belief—no difference, in the long run, than the
Establishments at Auschwitz and Theresienstad where the
Methods differed but the results were similar—kill for the
Belief that this would serve the nation—Kali has so many
Names—now in Bosnia it's being done on the same basis as
It has been done in Soweto, for so long—We believe, we
Believe—the Virgin Mary is no longer Virgin—the Star of
The Sea—Maris Stella is no longer there as the Protectress
Of sailors—old Gods, die, and Goddesses too—new ones
Are born—Science—Communism—all the beliefs for
Which we live or are put to death by, the ones in power—
Empowered by the System of Belief that happens to be
Operative at that time—the Ghost Dance and the charges
At Antietam into the cannon balls were not that
Disparate—South Central in flames, and Sarajevo in flames,
Beirut bombed, and the World Trade Center, bombed—
Mysteries—give us this day our daily ration of ammunitions,
Explosives, bombs, that we may serve you into eternity—
And the crusade at Acre believed as Lyndon Johnson
Believed when Vietnam was flowering—mysteries—why did
We go for all that shit McCarthy stirred up? Why does the
Aryan Nation in Pocatello provide pistols for target
Practice to its members with the targets in the form of black
Dummies with curly black hair, with others in the form of
The caricatures faithfully drawn of old hook-nosed Jews
Whose invention was first manifested in the Nazi comic books

Of not so long ago—mysteries all of them—our
Actions absolved by Mercury being in retrograde—by the
Forthcoming conjunction of Uranus and Neptune—
Hypnotized into consciousness—the Snake Clan at Hopi—
The acid hangovers from the Haight Ashbury—the Vestal
Virgins in the temple in Rome, not that different from what
Can be made out of the ruins of Machu Picchu—this
Recurring need for the idea of Virginity—never mind that
Jesus had an older brother, James, the Less, I believe thrown down
And over and out of the Wall of the Temple Mount—purification
—This appetite for that which lies there, just out of reach—
Out of touch—which makes us sweat for an idea—lust for
Marilyn Monroe and all her descendants—the centerfolds
Of our age—the ones we can have in mind but not in body
Or heart—a nation of intellectuals where the idea of
Madonna/sex becomes more important than the act
Itself—where we have become separated by thin rubber
Walls, from true contact with the mystery because of the
Fear of death from AIDS, from truth—always the shield—
Always the need to bury the spent fuel so it will not harm
Us for 10,000 years—mysteries all those hidden and those
That stalk the snipes on the walls—the J. Edgar Hoover
Line of crotchless panties to be marketed next month in all
The WalMarts of the nation—we trust—we believe—it says
So on our dollar bills—in our beds in the morning—in the
Bars at night—in front of the television—mysteries and all
Their coruscations. Who are we, that we are shaped and that
Our deeds are shaped by that which we believe—the human
Ability to love the greater mystery, reborn each time when
That luminous strength invades us and gives us the will and
Power to make things grow and happen—come back Maris
Stella, come back Marilyn, come back baby, come home.

Riff #5

Meditation

Sit in front of the tree, look at it, become the tree—not the
Allegorical tree, tree of life, family tree, pick a piñon to look
At and become that piñon, that ponderosa, that ancient
Apricot, young elm, cedar—that one tree! Learn to sit in
Front of, or slightly to the side of, one of those large rocks on
The way up to the ski basin or choose Black Mesa itself—
With the yellow flowers on top—become that rock, become
That mountain—and you will then stop—for clarity—but
Do not even dream of doing that, unless you have Ariadne's
Thread hidden in your palm or in your heart, so as, to be able
To find your way back to this life, this way of being—
Assuming this is the place you choose to be in—if not—
Then that thread of Ariadne's is excess baggage, ready for
Jettisoning, not valid for you, for the explorer who only
Wants to go forward, never to return—Varda's parable about
Cupid's arrow, taken over by city planners, to mark one way
Roads, traffic patterns that do not permit contrary traffic
—that arrow, that teaches us the way of love; released,
It hits home, released it travels to find the heart, released it
Makes mockery of distance, released it thinks its way into
Another consciousness, makes distances negligible and acts
As a catalyst does, never to let the components return to
Their original state—son of Sagittarius whose uncle,
Neptune's trident knows the same pointed logic that your
Arrows live by, son of Sagittarius waiting for Venus to rise
Out of the salt spume of her father's sea, creating the weather
Of the heart as well as the one of clouds, dangerous divider.
Trickster, maker of illusions, patron of all pharmaceuticals,
Intelligence made manifest through itself, teacher and
Avenger should anyone betray you and try to go back

Anywhere, back to school, back to the nest, back to a first
Love—it'll kill you, Varda said, laughing that month before
He died, falling out of the airplane that had brought him

Back to see an old love—they said it was the altitude
And his weak heart—Mexico City is only for the ones who
Can manage altitude and his heart could not—it was the
Going back, the attempt to re-create—creation the first
Time is tough enough—you can not go back.
We were given eyes in the front of our heads to look
Forward—not back—we are predators—the eyes forward—
Horses can look back—they are prey—look at your friends—
Their eyes will tell you—each time—prey or
Predator—predator or prey—we do not look back—
Forward—the long voyage that enables us to become tree,
To become rock, to become the other—Krishna Jee said, one
Could become the other, leaving the self, behind—the
Ultimate penetration, self-transmuted into another, without
An intervening death, rebirth, diapers, school, acne, shyness,
Growing up, talk to be right where you are and I, you—
You—me—thank you, that trip is not the one, take—love,
That tree, become that tree, look to the world and the
Seasons as if you were in fact, that tree, but return to the
Sentient being in love with the tree, the woman, the man,
The mountain, the moon, straight as arrow's flight, learning
Each time for the first time, the road forward into delight,
The smoke of fires, the awakening that comes with new
Beginnings, with dawns, and with the manifestation of hope.
The map-marker pointing forward. Going home.

Riff #6

Reality Check

Lovers seen in a Sushi bar, in Santa Fe, New Mexico one evening in the
Second week of January at the very beginning of the millennium on an
Evening that seems to be a winter's evening, though really appearing to be
Spring. They, the lovers, appear to be moving up toward the ceiling of
The interior that appears to be quite Japanese; he with his head arching
Around to kiss her in much the way Chagall appeared to be arching while
Kissing Maria, his bride, in that painting he did of their wedding. She, with
Her hair loose, full-lipped, and presenting herself to him as if they wee
Really nineteen and twenty-three, completely involved in the moment as
One can only be when in love, or in poetry when all else disappears. I then
Recognized Jim and Marilyn who, somehow, had become transfigured.
Yes, the old friends, Jim and Marilyn each of whom had full lives behind
Them, children, baggage, and whatnot, appearing as young lovers, in that
Restaurant, which if one chose to believe, was really in Japan, appearing to
Be owned by a tall eager American who had recently required all his sushi
Chefs to wear white shirts and dark, narrow ties, making them appear to
Be IBM salesmen from the sixties, eager to please, while Jim and Marilyn
Continued to float up there, near the ceiling, above the tables and the
Patrons, above the spicy yellowtail salads being prepared, and above the
Sushi platters being served, leaving the question open, as to the reality of
Each element, in that particular moment, as well as, the appearance of all the
Energy that had been utilized and expended by all concerned to be there at
That moment or to appear to be there, if one were to choose to do so. That
Whole cargo of people, the lovers, others not so engaged, the servers, the
Chefs, the scullions, the janitors and all those people behind them, the delivery
People, who had brought the fish a thousand miles inland from Seattle, the
Fishermen who had gone fishing and had apparently caught the fish,
Netted them and brought them ashore, the warehouse men and women on
The docks, and all the accounting and legal and inspection and even the
Licensing personnel, as well as, all the other support people who had all
Conspired, it appeared, to get Jim and Marilyn hovering over our table and
All the others too, all that Friday evening in mid-January, up there, up close
To the ceiling, in a sweet and daring exercise of loving, or at least appearing
To be loving, for all of us to see.

Riff #7

Mistakes

We've all made mistakes, little ones, big ones, even
Huge ones. Ezra Pound becoming a mouthpiece for Mussolini
For example—did not make his poetry less—but
Made things difficult—I sometimes think I should
Have gone to St. Elizabeth's to see him when
Ginsberg asked me to go with the gang, he had
Been putting together—*"That asshole?"* I said, *"don't*
"Count on me," turning away feeling righteous and
Stupid at the same time—After what we had
Been through, as my mother put it—now looking
At pictures of the old angry man, taken in Italy.
After he had been let out of the jail/hospital
In Washington to go back to Pisa, where he had
Been jailed, back to Venice, loving the things I had
Come to love, eating at the same tratoria my
Brother Mark would go to, still there, across from
The boatyard where they still make the black
Gondola, they've made there for centuries, wondering
About how mistakes can be set right thinking about
The way it had been fashionable for the good old boys,
Including his pal Eliot, the T.S. one, to be down on the Jews,
Of course—wondering about the brilliant invention of the
Confessional and the structure of belief systems. I look
Into the mirror, to see my own mistakes sidling up to
Me, wanting attention, while I turn away as fast
As possible, and make a run for the field, trusting
That they will in fact fall away, in time, in
Those huge spaces that hide behind
Mirrors, behind memories and behind the trees,
That make up the forest of our separate pasts.
That one check facilitated, that one DWI, that one
And the other ones, glossed-over, deleted, expunged
But still ingrained and part of the packet, the lot.
That which I carry, you carry south in New Mexico.
Down to Truth and Consequence and
Down to Tucumcari.

Riff #8

Risk

No—eight thousand times—it is not that I choose to live on
The edge—that edge—the knife's blade—the place where
The drop to one side, vertical into space, while on the
Other, it slips down sheets of ice with no soft snow to land
On, down there, far down where the basalt rocks begin to
Poke their gnarled hands out of the smooth ice—
Waiting—no—more than a thousand times a thousand—
No—but you say you see me there, and I must have chosen,
And the answer is as double-edged as the sword I have been
Walking, because I do not know of any other way to get
THERE—all the fairy tales we were told as children, have
The same storyline—don't you remember? The one that
Takes you through the dark wood, full of monsters, to get
There? The one that makes you sneak by the sleeping ogre's
Lair, to get the princess, the treasure? A lot of Homer's
Stories are about that same edge, and we say it was the
Dawn of literature! The beginning of our western world!
Priam, Achilles, all that band of heroes! Sacking and
Looting, and raping and killing, in such heroic fancies—and
What's going on in Bosnia, is just more of the same—
Amplified by modern technology, that multiplies the
Effectiveness, and the numbers, even though it's still one
Cock at a time if it's rape, or if it's dawn—no, again, no—I
Choose to get there—I choose to hang on when I slip
Instead of letting go—the way it was five years ago, when I
Fell and managed, by the proverbial hair, to hang on—let
Go, let go, everyone shouted—we want to see the splash—
Everyone except those few who are still here on the edge
With me, surprised we've come so far—even my son, whose
Down to earthiness will have no patience with metaphor,
Goes to the top of the world on his mountain bike—
Kashgar, then over the Himalayas, the pass of the Old Silk
Road is at 16,000 feet. He and his buddy leave to go on up
To 19,000 just to see the view and then back down to
16,000, to go on to get there—and he says, the same thing

About choosing to be on the edge—denying it—does
Repetition justify it? Was my father's living, on-the-edge,
That made it possible for us to get out of China, in time?
Was it my mother's ability to navigate the weather of the
World, that made it possible for us to get there? To San
Francisco, fifty-two years ago, this week? The edge is
The only way to get there, I was told, when I asked,
Because, it was to have been Krishmamurti's last talk, at the
Oaks, and no way to celebrate the clarity of that man's
Message than to go beyond. I thought but I was very young,
Then, having come into new life, not knowing it then, as I
Am doing the same thing, now, on the edge, answering no—
A thousand times again, no—I do not like it, but it's the
Only way I know to get, there—knife's edge—falling—
Catching myself on that branch, jutting out of the rockface
—Answering that call—going on still, going—beginning
To begin, once again, a thousand and one and two and
Three nights, days, times, changes, all in the name
Of persistence—that which brought us here to this lifetime.
Place and moment; time as always the only
Irreplaceable increment. This moment.

Riff #9

Bon Appetit

Controlled by our appetites, not differing so much from the horses
Down in the pasture by the river, we remember we were prey once
Instead of the predators we've become. We go from meal to meal,
Doing all the daily that needs doing in order to feed ourselves, to
Feed the children and eventually all those out there that need our
Help, our hands, our hearts.

We build freeways, bridges and cathedrals. We design and launch
Ships that take us up as far as and beyond the moon and build
Engines of destruction that can and may yet undo the work of aeons
Of evolution and the quest for good. We find ways of making up to
Each other once there's been a war, a fight—even a divorce—and we
Find it appropriate to work it out for the greater good—but for Some
of us it's still impossible to break bread together without Calling up
all the curses that our ancestors hurled at each other.

We eat, we gain and lose weight, look at starving children on the
Telly without missing even one quick bite. We drink what's out There
and advertised so that we too may look like the prince or Princess of
the moment. We send food with our good wishes to Celebrate a tribal
rite and occasionally, suffering from an attack of Guilt, we go down
to the kitchen where the homeless come to feed And ladle out the
spoonfuls of that which Is too much for us, still Controlled by our
appetites.

We raise our glasses to toast a victory, our way of counting coup. We
Remember friends no longer with us, we even find religious solace
Eating the body and the blood of God in rituals celebrated around
The world. We eat and, in between the eating, we manage to find
Time to dream, to make love and have the children that we'll teach to
Sow and plant and reap so that they too will have enough to eat and
To share with friends while dreams are relegated to those moments
In between our meals, or between the phone calls that will tell us
Whether there's enough that's been put away to keep us safe,
Well-fed and happy for a time.

Riff #10

About A Woman

Not about any woman, and yet about all women,
At the same time, so that they can and will and do,
Become that woman, who is that woman who fulfills, filling
The whole world so full, it spills right over into beauty with
Breath and breadth, as bounty to bless and justify, the
Existence of all the saints of all religions making out of the
Fiction of heaven, tangible reality . . . That woman for whom
All the plays have been written, produced, performed,
Perceived and praised, and damned as well. That woman who
Is herself, without youth or age, who is there when while
Giving, receives, remembers, and retrieves with hope, even for
Those without hope, all of the helpless . . The one whose
Name is both, Mary and Maria, whose name is Kwan Yin as
Well as Isis, and Astarte, and Andromeda, as well the one who
Shares, shines, and sparkles while furnishing reasons to build
The house, light the fire, plow the fields, put out to sea,
Haul the nets in, and soar into the sky, while she trusts,
Believes, has confidence, and faith in, the outcome. She is that
Very one whose thought becomes arrow and target, both at the
Same time, instant and second, who holds the universe in
Balance and beauty, becoming laughter and lightness, singing
In the light of the dawn before sunrise. That woman who is
Sister of your own heart's self, while also Lilith at the identical
Moment, apricot-skinned, sweet, and salt sweated, at the same
Time, in whom trust and reverence rise, as if summoned by
Star or by Reason. That one again, who measures eternity in
an Instant, and light years with her outstretched arm, who is as
Gentle as cats are— at evening light . . Woman of clouds, of
Wind and of salt spume, the one you have known and loved
And been with, without knowing her, without being fully
Aware of her marrow, her scent, her knees and divisions. She is
That one woman who becomes song in the quiet of dusk, and
Is also the stamping of feet on floors that clack and resound,
With the chords of guitars, and the clapping and clicking and

Laughter and challenge of fingers and thumbs snapping.
While becoming tambourine, castanet, ring cymbal and drum,
Flirting with brilliance and sparkles and the bang and slap of
Heels, brought sharp to the floor with a crack, echoing the
Snap of the whip, of the cape, of the fist brought hard into
Palm and the toe tapping, drumming. While she comes out of
The dark into the beam of light shining again, becoming
Moth, dream, memory and vengeance, who is out and about,
The touch of thigh, touched by thigh, of hands touching hips,
Of flesh and of home lost, and alone in the night,
Frightened of phantasm who drift in unannounced, ready to
Pounce and devour. What she is about, this woman, who
Suddenly turns away becoming like ice as defense because the
Color is wrong or the lamp is not right or the paint is still wet
And the bet has been lost and no matter the cost she turns and
We go, no we run, no we fly after her to say that it was all a
Mistake, a fault in the doing, the reason for undoing all the
Plans, so that in fact, the boat was missed but we got to port
Somehow because she is what she is about. This woman who
Sings in the morning and touches herself with the pleasures of
Feathers and sunlight of dawning and dreaming this one who
Is all mother and sister and daughter and daughter and sister
And mother in turn who turns into gentle and sweetness and
Caring while also daring to turn into star flesh and firelight
And the dancing of waters, of swallows at evening and of
Finches at dawning as the sun rises and shines its way into
Corners that had been hidden, rushing the dark light for all of
Us as only she has ever known how she who is there when
She's needed, who is offered the world as a token of all the
Great treasures within it, who is given the rainbow as a token
Of color, and of all that is yet to be found, becoming aware
That she is both a part and a party to all that is pleasure.. .
Triune in her measures, with Spirit and wisdom and body all
Present, who sings and who listens, who writes and who reads,
Who caresses the breeze of desire as well as the one of

Jaguar and the song of the thrush, always ready to find and to
Be found, unclothed, waiting for the caress of the beloved
While caressing him, who teaches by being and is at the same
Time, herself, the teaching, the dance, the music, the starlight
And dew, while all the while she who is the other part of my
Heart and its beating, the breath of my lung and my skins own
Touch. this woman who is herself and no other, not even
Similar to all of the others I had loved before, almost as
Practice for this time, this moment, this touch of the sun's
Traveling, with its rays breaking through clouds on their way
To the Piñon, as the mountains rise to give it good fortune so
That this woman rises again each day with the dawning, with
Feathers, with touching, with all that is there in the world
Because this woman is about learning and teaching and
Feasting and fasting and dancing and falling and rising as the
Wings of the eagle that touch you and hold you as you fly over
Mountains. . .and also about her inventions, her treasures and
Laughter and also about the calm that pervades her, the one
That makes sleeping beside her the rest of all time, the one
Who wakes you with teasing and softness, who is all that she
Is because she is that one who is.

Riff #11

Billboards

What's to do with them?
Put them where people can see them as they go by?
Have them printed on cheap newsprint and dropped off
    by acolytes as they go door to door?
Grind them up and put them in pills to be put in bottles
    to be sold in Health Food Stores!
Chew them up and spit them out into vats of LSD
    to then be dumped into the reservoirs of city waters across
    the land.
Tear them into electronic waves that would be broadcast
    as the subtext for the CNNs, the Oprahs and the Lettermans.
Send them into the heavens to meet the light of Betelgeuse
    so as to hitch a ride back to everywhere.
Too complicated, too difficult perhaps, so then let's just buy some
    Billboards and set them up everywhere we can
To ask those questions no one ever does, to give the
    answers we all need, to sing the songs
That people want their bones to want, and to
                 INSIST
On being their own bone selves, their fires and their time.
That's what, that's what
That's what to do with them!

Riff #12

Directions

Where do you think we're supposed to go now
Into the air, into the questioning sea, into philosophy?

Reaching out to a reservoir of courage when the strength
    has dribbled out and the gauge shows empty
I summon all my familiars to this game
Unfolding panoply, staking out the turf, making
Mock medieval logic the stage designer much as
Those people did during the War when Bobby Helpman
And Olivier rebuilt Henry the Fifth into a parable
Of courtly games that came out well for England
For Harry and of course St. George, not yet then
Revised out of the canon, and so made it all
Ring true as if the bells ringing were truly bells
And not the electronic imitations that ring
Out from the Campanile in the rain or the ones that sound
Out from onion domes when Eisenstein's Nevsky
    was done foretelling the fate of those Teutonic Knights
Outside of Novgorod.

                    And it is, as my son says,
Another example of the intellectualization of this time.
No longer the Kantian "Ding an Sich" —
The thing in itself — but the idea of the thing —
The idea of sex in the videos proliferating across the world
And in Guccione's and Heffner's magazines with their airbrushed packages
The idea of riches in the hedge funds and the
NASDAQ quotes, the ideas of the Coptic church
Revivified once again into the Politics of Meaning.

                    And you over there unreachable
And so tantalizing to see you walk down the TV runway
Yes, strutting down the runway of your desire impaling

Every look thrown your way on the spearpoints of your glances.

Will you continue this continuity, extension, enhancement
    of your need to be admired on the runways
Of Milan, of Paris, of London and New York until all
    the flashbulbs flash, all the videos turn into stills
You can paste into your albums for verification
    so that you know yourself to be alive as a
Result of all that adulation?

                        Of course you will,
And pick up a haiku or two along the way while
    being your most seduisante in the
Reflections we get to see as you disappear, again
    and once again, the idea more
Attractive than the sweat, the smells, the
functions that make the body that which
IT IS.

    No veils, no springtime lilac in the water
Which is spritzed about, no seduction, no
No. 5, no Poême sold in fancy shapes of glass, no,
Nothing but the smells of semen and of being
Together in the bed to rise again on the third day
And not before.

    Of course it's Easter we dream about, and the
Resurrection lends itself to as many interpretations
As there are tesserae in the mosaic floor of
The Holy Sepulchre. We bury and we rise,
Again and once more, and once more
Again, thinking it's us and our appetites.
NO!

It's that old drive. The one that Goodall spends
   her life researching in DARK AFRICA. The one that drove
Roy Chapman Andrews out into Mongolian deserts
   to find its eggs. Cocksure, that's what
WE ARE!
         Have been and will be until this
Place blows up courtesy of WIPP or by itself.

No ephemerae, we say. No Golden Monarchs
   crowding round the trees out on the point, no more connections
Between Eleusis and the Haight by way of ergot
   that made it clear in all the rainbow colors, the exstasy
The wind, or God's own promise to Noah that
   day when JHVH knew he had overshot the mark!!

We do want everything. The rock and the hard place too,
Where the petroglyphs give evidence. We want
Assurance. We want to know the way to go
Because it is our right, we say. We will
Bow down as we always have, to Pope,
To Emperor, To Mammon or to the Stars
And bring the children up in awe of that
One certainty we choose, kissing the feet
Of this Sultan or that one.

"Oh, come and dance with us in the springtime grasses," say,
I hear them call even in this winter's time
And hear them as I've heard them sing
   for all my years. Hang in there, it's only
One more winter to live through before the
   roses and the daffodils come up from
Southern spheres to dance us through
   the mirror into our own sweet Wondertime.
   WE ARE!
         WE ARE!

Riff #13

Wrap

How do you think we're supposed to wrap it up now?
With butcher paper and duct tape, with sheepskins and wire?
With aluminum foil all crinkled up pretty, with an Ite Missa Est?
How can you sleep in the light of the TV set whose eye sees Hutus
And Tutsis compete with last year's equivalent of the Serbs and the Muslims
And the Croats and the Desparacidos of the year before as if
This competition mattered to anyone but the protagonists themselves?
Why don't they bring a child who has just lost its mother to
Any one of the Poetry Workshops to be interviewed in its tears by all
Those future MFAs or even a mother who has lost her children
As an alternate choice so that scripts could be set up as versions of
THE REAL THING?

                              Take me down to the river, take me
To the Autumn meadow where there are cornstalks still on the ground
Take me to the place in the Bosque where the sunflowers carpeted the ground
Only yesterday and gave back the sunlight for all of us and tell me
How it is that we made it all the way to Here and to Now.

                                            INSIST
On ambivalence and you might have a chance. Bite the bullet
When they saw your foot off to make you well. Go into the marketplace
As soon as you've come from the cave in the mountain. Be rich
In the moment and poor in Eternity or flip it and make it
Go the other way for today and tomorrow. Act as if you had
All of time in your pocket to spend at the same time as you felt
The last dime of a minute slipping away from your hand but always
Insist on the moment, insist as the peach insists on becoming
Itself and there might be a place at the table.

                                          YESTERDAY
Oswald shot Kennedy, thirty-three years ago. Forty-three years ago
A courts martial convened at Hamilton Field to determine
Whether I had been prematurely Anti-Fascist and a threat

To the State. Fifty-three years ago I sailed off to the Pacific as
An ordinary seaman anxious to do something to help in the War and
Thirty-three years ago my daughter was born and three years ago
My face in the mirror became that of a stranger I've been
In the process of getting to know. All these threes on the same
Branch of the tree, all leaves coexisting, waving at each other
As the Autumn breezes blow and it's one moment only and
Yet it's a life insisting on its singularity while being the same
As that of all the other leaves.

                         TODAY, like the crest of the wave
Or rather the curl just before the crest that brings the surfer
In to the beach stays in the same place while moving
Everything along, surfers, help, light, sand, water, salt
And all their collocations and interactions. My memory
Holds what it can, stays in the same place and yet moves
Up and down like the water in the wave.

                                    "Sex and love are
Not the same thing "—Duchamp said—and yet *"both are to be*
Considered as worthy of a place at the table"—Varda said.
"If one is the package and the other the packaging which
One is which?" Walter Landor asked.

                              Consider the old
Whose memories get chucked into dustbins or get discovered by
Those who make a living = present—life. Now out of the
Gathering of old sketches, paint boxes, pieces of what is now past
To turn into collectibles—there, that old frame burnished —
Such a beautiful present—thank you, darling—you're such
A dear—expensive—expansive—
                         TOMORROW

Yes,

       . . .TOMORROW, promised to no one,
All of them, each one of us has had and squandered, oh how
We've waited for them, planned for them, saved for them,
Fought for them, prayed for them and then, in spite of
The prayers, have them turn into something else causing
The dedication in the book, the snapshots with everyone's
Eyes turning red in the picture, the ring, the trip to New
York or New Guinea, the Emergency Room and then the
Arrangements with the Mortuary, the Bank and the
Salvation Army while the rest of the world gets written up
In the paper and somewhere, someone one knows gets a prize,
Goes to jail or wakes with delight in the arms of the beloved.

No way out of it until one's out of it! Hop skip and scramble
And make a run for it while standing still. Tell the children
It isn't so, that seventeen people in New York control the shape
And content of all the News that's fit to Eat in all the continents
And there is no name yet for this kind of Archy in the Book.

Perhaps when we go to the Yucatan in the New Year, where
Clear sweet water empties out directly under limestone cliffs
Into the sea we'll find an answer and get a drink.

Hold me for pleasure, not for gain, we'll be together, in smoke,
We'll be together in rain, but hold the moment while
It holds us; let's stay together or we'll miss the bus!

Victor di Suvero was born in Italy in 1927, grew up in China and came to the United States with his family as a political refugee in early 1941. When the Second World War broke out he was too young to be accepted in the Armed Forces, so he went to sea as a Merchant Seaman when he was 16. After the war he went to the University of California at Berkeley where he received his B.A. in Political Science in 1949. At Berkeley he had been the editor of the *Occident*, the literary magazine of the University and won the *Ina Coolbrith Prize* for Poetry in that year.

He then went into business and established Design and Color Service in San Francisco in 1951 and then went on to become a Real Estate and Mortgage Broker and Developer of real estate and mining projects for the next 32 years.

His publications include, *Salt and the Heart's Horizons,* Greenwood Press 1951, *Sight Poems*, Stolen Paper Editions, 1962, *San Francisco Poems* and *The Net*, 1987, *Tesuque Poems*, 1993, *Naked Heart*, 1997. He has edited *¡Saludos!* the first bilingual collection of the poetry of New Mexico, all from Pennywhistle Press which he established in 1986.

As a poetry activist he served as a Director of the National Poetry Association for four years in which position he participated in the management of the 2nd National Poetry Week in San Francisco in 1987. After moving to New Mexico in 1988, di Suvero became one of the Founders of PEN New Mexico, of the New Mexico Book Association and of the Poetry Center of New Mexico.

Di Suvero now lives in la Villita, New Mexico on a ranch on the Rio Grande, halfway between Santa Fe and Taos and continues to write and work in community affairs in the area.

Publisher's Note

PENNYWHISTLE PRESS CELEBRATES THE MILLENNIUM!

Established in 1986 the Press has grown, maintaining a lively conversation between the authors it has published and their readers as it hopes to, continue relating to, and with the poets, writers, critics, reviewers and readers of the future.

The Press has expanded its outreach and its books are distributed by Small Press Distribution of Emeryville, California among various other distributors and wholesalers.

Pennywhistle's latest collection of distinguished and important poetry underlines the commitment the Press has made to share a wide range of voices, presented in a responsible manner to a public seriously interested in good work and an expansion of the landscape of poetry.

ρ

Bosque Redondo by Keith Wilson

This collection is an important selection collection of poems whose theme is the evocative power of memory. In the hands of the poet memory becomes the catharsis that opens up the world of childhood, a space the poet must revisit. Noted voice of the Post Beat era, *Keith Wilson*, friend of *Charles Olson, Sid Corman, Robert Duncan, Robert Creeley and Gary Snyder*, recognized the responsible voice of his time in New Mexico and in the West. Rudolfo Anaya contributes a fine introduction.

108 pages $12.00, ISBN 0-938631-28-4

Blood Trail by Florence McGinn

The cross-cultural currents that have enriched American writing in the later part of the 20th century continue to be part of the literary scene today. *Florence McGinn's* work continues that cross-cultural adventure. Her poetry, crafted with care for the detail of her Chinese heritage, reaches into our consciousness with current American scenes and with language that touches our hearts. The book has an introduction by Victor di Suvero.

108 pages $12.00, ISBN 0-938631-34-9

Harvest Time by Victor di Suvero

A gathering, a dozen years of writing around and about the poet's moving to the high desert of the Southwest, home to the crowded histories of Indian, Hispanic and Anglo settlers all of whom have called the same stretches of eroded sandstone, harshly cut arroyos and fertile fields and orchards their home.

148 pages $15.00, ISBN 0-938631-36-5

Voces del Rincon/Voices from the Corner by Mike Sutin

A collection of poetry mexpressed by the personae assumed by the poet, addressing issues pertinent to life lived in the corners of the poet touches on histories of the area, as well as, current events as perceived by participants, and onlookers in the New Mexico landscape crossed by the network of the highways of today. Introduction by Victor di Suvero

112 pages $15.00, ISBN 0-938631-33-0

naked Heart by Victor di Suvero

This collection of *Victor di Suvero's* as poetry is a compendium of poems which dance between the wise old street experiences of San Francisco to the delicate and sensual places we learn to honor through love and time. This selection makes the case for love exciting, erotic, evocative and thoughtful...all at the same time. Poet James Broughton said that, *"di Suvero is valiant to take the risk of disrobing his heart—it's the only way to be a genuine poet."* And poet and Nuyorican Cafe founder, *Bob Holman*, has this to say: *"When you listen to the beat of di Suvero's collection, naked Heart, you will hear yourself falling in love with poetry."*

80 pages $12.00, ISBN 0-938631-28-4

Hooplas! by James Broughton

Is a collection of festive tributes to friends and intimates of the author, who salutes their talents and personalities with song, fanfare and wit. These odes for odd occasions are offered in praise of friendship, in memory of merriment, and in awe of love.The poet died in 1999 after completing this special tribute to his many friends.

93 pages $8.95, ISBN 0-938631-02-0

Pennywhistle Press is in the process of developing a series of bilingual Anthologies. First in this series is:

¡Saludos!

¡Saludos! Poemas de Neuvo Mexico is the first bilingual anthology of the poetry of New Mexico. Sixty six fine Native American, Hispanic and Anglo poets share their experience of the Land of Enchantment with clear and heartfelt poems that sing! Poets represented in this strong and unique collection include *Miriam Sagan, Jim Sage, Leo Romero, Charles Bell, Greg Glazner, Peggy Pond Church, Luci Tapahonso and Joy Harjo,* among others.

290 pages $15.00, ISBN 0-938631-33-0

Anthologies of the current poetry of Chile, Cuba and Italy are currently in the development stage.

Pennywhistle Press initiated its chapbook series in 1988. Sine then, it has published 18 individual chapbooks featuring the work of a poet with an introduction by a peer and for a critic to place the author and his work in perspective. The individual chapbooks, now in print are listed below. Details regarding the chapbook series follows:

The Press currently offers the following titles in its Chapbook Series:

ρ

The Blue Series

Sublunary by Jorge H, -Aigla's
Writing goes to the heart of experience with clarity, illuminating truth as perceived by him. Taking his cues from the dark side of life, Aigla reaches out with caring insight. Introduction by Charles G. Bell.
32 pages $6.00, ISBN 0-938631-07-1

Full Turn by Sarah Blake
Her book exposes the sacred territory of domestic blood connections, of love and family–demonstrating how ordinary life has a tendency to trap and bind. *Blake* roots herself in the present and struggles with ghosts of the past, convincingly adept at being both here and there at once. Introduction by Dorianne Laux.
32 pages $6.00, ISBN 0-938631-05-5

Further Sightings & Conversations by Jerome Rothenberg
He has an overriding preoccupation with seeing. His work comes from a need for concentrated visionary representation. Shaman and High Priest of language, he sings as he explores and blesses the world. Introduction by Michael Palmer.

32 pages $6.00, ISBN 0-938631-03-9

The Fields by Richard Silberg
His work is spare and complicated and speaks to the process of personal discovery. His brilliant resolutions bring one home. Introduction by Joyce Jenkins.
32 pages $6.00, ISBN 0-938631-05-5

Who is Alice? by Phyllis Stowell
Her preoccupation with the need for a common language between the sexes generates a passionately argued sequence of poems about silence. Introduction by Sandra Gilbert
32 pages $6.00, ISBN 0-938631-04-7

The Sum Complexities of the Humble Field by Viola Weinberg
She offers a poetry of the sensual that can be tasted and touched. At the same time, she presents her world with discipline and mathematical precision. Introduction by Mary Mackey.
32 pages $6.00, ISBN 0-938631-06-3

The Red Series

No Golden Gate for Us by Francisco X. Alarcon
His poems give simultaneous voice to the pain and humor of the desperado who has seen and felt too much and to the quiet understanding that comes with wisdom. Introduction by Felipe Herrera.
32 pages   **$6.00, ISBN 0-938631-16-0**

Tesuque Poems by Victor di Suvero
He embraces a world grounded in arroyos and trees, lightning storms and streams. Complicated and thought-provoking, his poetry celebrates survival while praising the phenomena of existence. Introduction by Pierre Delattre.
32 pages   **$6.00, ISBN 0-938631-17-9**

Hardwired for Love by Judyth Hill
She takes her readers on a lyrical roller coaster ride through ancient past toward a luminous future. Her essential message is direct, and her laughter, sensuality, intelligence and exuberance infuses her work with love, spiritual awareness and aesthetic discipline. Introduction by Miriam Sagan.
32 pages   **$6.00, ISBN 0-938631-13-6**

The Width of a Vibrato by Edith A. Jenkins
She writes a poetry of affirmation that begins with awareness of loss and is dwelt upon until the poet is able to transmute that loss into affirmation. Introduction by Robert Glück.
32 pages   **$6.00, ISBN 0-938631-10-1**

Portal by Joyce Jenkins
Her poetry offers readers a rare combination of playfulness spoken with wisdom—showing a complex nature devoid of bitterness. Introduction by Carolyn Kizer.
32 pages   **$6.00, ISBN 0-938631-18-7**

Falling Short of Heaven by Susan Lummis
Her work is the quintessence of a high strung, highly sensitive and wildly intelligent woman's attempt to get along in this big, bad world. Her poetry is written with a theatrical feel that makes it seem lived in. Introduction by Austin Straus.
32 pages   **$6.00, ISBN 0-938631-12-8**

The Green Series

Where you've Seen Her by Grace Bauer

She has earned her reputation for a clear and incisive use of language. Ms. Bauer illuminates her subject matter with an honesty all too rare in today's world. Introduction by Robin Becker.

32 pages $6.00, ISBN 0-938631-11-X

Decoy's Desire by Kerry Shawn Keys

His appreciation of the natural beauty of his world–specifically that lush hillside in Perry Co., Pennsylvania–surfaces throughout this collection. Introduction by Gerald Stern.

32 pages $6.00, ISBN 0-938631-14-4

What Makes a Woman Beautiful by Joan Logghe

She shares a voice as ancient and wise as time. With gleaming syntax honed to perfection, Ms. Logghe's women–and men–live their everyday realities and how "beauty" abides and sustains. Introduction by Jim Sagel.

32 pages $6.00, ISBN 0-938631-15-2

Chaos Comics by Jack Marshall

His work is sensual and intense; his supple, possibilities of perception with a philosophy that is breathtaking in its audacity and scope. Introduction by Morton Marcus.

32 pages $6.00, ISBN 0-938631-25-X

Between Landscapes by Wai-Lim Yip

He has created a magical, musical scale that enchants, soothes and lulls, rises and falls, as it simultaneously plunges us into the beauty and power of the terrible and sublime cycles of nature. Introduction by Jerome Rothenberg.

32 pages $6.00, ISBN 0-938631-24-1

Still The Sirens by Dennis Brutus

His poems take us from the rigors of apartheid to the bestiality of imprisonment and from the desolation of exile to those moments of recognition and acknowledgement that make the struggle worthwhile. Introduction by Lamont B. Steptoe.

32 pages $6.00, ISBN 0-938631-09-8

Sextet One

The first anthology in Pennywhistle's new series. This volume presents the work of six separate and distinct poets with each presentation containing an introduction by a noted critic or poet, a photo of the author and a collection of the poet's most recent work–a wonderful way to bring six new friends into one's life! This volume presents *Kim Addonizio, Tom Fitzsimmons, Harry Lawton, Annamaria Napolitano, Doren Robbins and Ruth Stone, with introductions by Dorianne Laux, Victor di Suvero, Maurya Simon, Pierre Saint-Amand, Philip Levine and Rebecca Seiferle.*

226 pages $17.50, ISBN 0-938631-27-6

Ordering Information

Call your order to 505-982-0066
Email: PennywhistleBook@aol.com
or fax it to 505-982-8116
or write to: PENNYWHISTLE PRESS
Post Office Box 734, Tesuque, New Mexico 87574